CARDIFF
THOSE CRUEL &
SAVAGE STREETS

A selection of cases from Cardiff Police archives
from Victorian times to the 1970s

John F. Wake

CARDIFF – THOSE CRUEL AND SAVAGE STREETS
A selection of cases from Cardiff police archives from Victorian times to the 1970s

© 2017 John F. Wake, cover deisgn © 2017 David Norrington
© Photography, illustrations, and diagrams supplied by the following sources, gratefully acknowledged by the author:

Butetown History Arts Centre (BHAC): p.15
Cardiff Libraries: front cover x 3, pp. 21, 25, 29, 48, 61, 73, 86, 98, 134, 147, 153, 156, 164, 165, 210, 211
CCPR Archive: front cover x2, p.23
Glamorgan Archive: front cover
Welsh Newspapers Online: pp. 54, 57x4, 133, 177x2

Martine Lloyd: p.45
Ross Mather: p.13, front cover
David Norrington pp. 116, 119x2
Mike O'Sullivan: pp. 39, 69
Dai Thomas: pp. 105, 111x2, back cover, front cover
John Wake: front cover, pp. 12, 16, 25, 34, 49, 114, 124, 159, 191, 197
Paul Welbeloved: front cover, p.26

The Author asserts the moral right to be identified as the author of this work. All rights reserved. This book is protected under the copyright laws of the United Kingdom. Any reproduction or other unauthorised use of the material or artwork herein is prohibited without the express written permission of the Publisher.

British Library Cataloguing in Publication Data.
A catalogue record for this book is available from the British Library.

No part of this book may be reproduced, stored in a retrieval system, or transmitted in any form or by any means, electronic, electrostatic, magnetic tape, mechanical, photocopying, recording or otherwise, without the written permission of the Publisher.

First published in the United Kingdom by Wordcatcher Publishing, Cardiff, UK in 2017

Republished independently, 2022
ISBN: 9798438206514

Category: History / Crime, Social

THIS BOOK IS DEDICATED
TO THE MEMORY OF
POLICE CONSTABLE WILLIAM PERRY
OF THE CARDIFF BOROUGH POLICE,
WHO WAS STABBED TO DEATH
IN THE WESTGATE HOTEL
ON 31st DECEMBER, 1872.

(HIS KILLER THEN STABBED HIMSELF,
SUSTAINING INJURIES FROM WHICH HE DIED).

Bill Perry was a police officer doing his duty.
An unassuming, ordinary, and long-forgotten man,
who gave his life whilst serving his community.

"I have not personally suffered from the deprivations, the bitterness and sorrow which bring so many men and women to a realisation of social injustice."
Emmeline Pankhurst

To be accused of something you have not done is unjust.
To be arrested for something you have not done is aggravated injustice.
To be executed for something you have not done is the ultimate injustice.

Social injustice isn't governed by law, but by the abuse of power, and may be more insidious and more dangerous than any miscarriage of the law.

Make your own mind up when reading these cases.
Was justice served in every case?

CONTENTS

Introduction 1

CHAPTER ONE
Policing the streets through time 3

- MORGUES AND INQUESTS 4
- STATION LIFE 7
- SEIGE MENTALITY 8
- EARLY DETECTIVE DEPARTMENT 8
- BEHIND CLOSED DOORS, TIME STOOD STILL 9
- BOBBIES ON BIKES 10
- POLICE ON FIRE DUTY 11
- POLICE POWERS 12
- STREET ARRESTS 12
- BLACK MARIAS 13
- SUBSISTENCE 14

CHAPTER TWO
Street life 17

- THE MOST VIOLENT STREET IN CARDIFF 17
- WORKING GIRLS 18
- THE CATHAYS INCIDENT 18
- DOWN AND OUTS 21
- ARRESTS OF VAGRANTS 21
- PUBS AND DEMOLITION 22
- LODGING HOUSES 25
- WANDER TO NEWTOWN 25
- THE LAST STOWAWAY ARREST 26
- THE DETECTIVE DEPARTMENT'S LAST DAYS 27
- THE LAST BLACK AND WHITE MUGSHOTS 27
- AND FINALLY… 28

CHAPTER THREE
Ripper victim: the murder of Mary Jane Kelly 29

CHAPTER FOUR
'The dreadful Canton husband murder' 37

CHAPTER FIVE
The forgotten stories of long-forgotten people 49
- ADELINE AMY DAVIES, 1902 49
- WICKED WILLY WILSON, 1896 51
- THE MAN WHO WOULD BE KING, 1861 53
- NEIGHBOURHOOD WATCH, CANTON-STYLE, 1855. 56
- THE ATTEMPTED MURDER OF 57
- THE REVEREND FATHER 57
- MICHAEL GAVIN GARELLI 57

CHAPTER SIX
The Llanrumney Hall murder 63

CHAPTER SEVEN
Debtors: the painful demise of William Jenkins 91

CHAPTER EIGHT
The short and brutal life of PC John Henry Kingdom 95

CHAPTER NINE
Hard times for women – baby abandonment and murder 111

- THE DINGLE DEATH 113
- THE HARROWING STORY OF THE GRANGETOWN SERVANT-GIRL 120
- THE ROATH MURDER, HELEN STREET 123
- ANOTHER DAY, ANOTHER CHILD 128
- A HUSSY OR VICTIM? MARY PETERSON MAHONEY 129

CHAPTER TEN
Harry Houdini in Cardiff Magistrates Court 137

CHAPTER ELEVEN
Cardiff's wildest publican 143

- MAD JACK'S ARREST SHEET 150
- MAD JACK MATTHEWS STANDS FOR THE COUNCIL 153
- A TYPICAL MAD JACK MATTHEWS ARREST AND COURT CASE 162
- CONTEMPORARIES OF MAD JACK: SAMUEL WILLIAMS AND PHILIP RICHARDS 167

CHAPTER TWELVE
"Revelation after revelation." The Splott baby farmer 171

CHAPTER THIRTEEN
The murder of William George Webb (11 months) 181

CHAPTER FOURTEEN
The 1975 Food College murder **187**

CHAPTER FIFTEEN
Llanishen (1844): the death of Elizabeth Sullivan **197**

APPENDIX
Tiger Bay Gold **205**

ACKNOWLEDGEMENTS **207**

Introduction

There can be no similarities between a constable walking his Cardiff beat in 1865 and one walking his Cardiff City beat a hundred years later in 1965, can there? A century of wars and civilisation must surely have changed the office of constable and his beat duties beyond recognition?

It is beyond my belief that in Cardiff in 1919, one year after the end of World War I, there were more than twenty multi-millionaires walking the streets. In those days a million pounds was a breath-taking amount of personal money. The Lord Mayor appealed for a charitable fund to be set up of just half a million pounds to look after the impoverished, the needy, and the disabled. The streets were populated with beggars. Something had to be done, but not much was.

The storylines of the rich and poor in Edwardian Cardiff must make powerful reading. Their witness died with them though. However, over the years there are compelling stories that are documented and can be told, referencing evil people, good people, sad people: the famous and the infamous of Cardiff.

We walk today where the rich, the poor, the sad, and the bad walked in a Cardiff of the past. We walk the streets blissfully unaware of whose footsteps we are walking in. The thousands of constables who have walked that way before us. What stories they could tell.

Cardiff's growth was phenomenal. In 1801 there were 1,870 inhabitants, in 1831 there were 6,187, in 1861 it had risen to 32,954, and in 1901 it was a staggering 164,333. Over one century a growth of nearly 1,000%.

Within that growth there was a startling figure. In the mid-19th century one in four babies died before their first birthday. Infant death was commonplace in the cruel and impoverished world of the back streets. Malnutrition and disease were the main contributors to their deaths.

Womanby Street runs between the areas of Quay Street and Castle Street as it has done for over a millennia. One can only imagine the hundreds of thousands of people who have walked that way over the years. Vikings, Normans, Royalists, Roundheads, etc. It is a fair bet that all of the people in this book had walked Womanby Street at some time of their lives.

Womanby Street, 2017. Some of the original early buildings still stand. The 18th century Globe Hotel *is on the left.*

The tragic lives of most Cardiff people are not known, their lives lost in obscurity, their stories never written in history. It seems only the rich and the famous courted positive headlines, and the only time the working classes came into view of the media was when they came before the law courts, and when they did this, it was usually dramatic.

CHAPTER ONE

Policing the streets through time

Cardiff Borough Police officer, 1890s

In 1895 it was gas that lit the town's streets and some of its residences. Gas lighting brought some illumination to the main thoroughfares in Cardiff but one can imagine not much.

The back alleys, the little side streets and dockland areas, were plunged into blackness as the sun set. Consequently, as soon as the night drew in, Cardiff's back streets were a dangerous place to be. Rogues, vagabonds, unfortunates, and the impoverished, trawled the back alleys and undertook opportunist thefts and robberies. Sailors were out looking for 'girls' to party with, girls were out looking for sailors to rob or get paid for sex. The back-street pubs were full to bursting with dockers, sailors, locals, and women drinking themselves into oblivion.

The fun stopped as soon as the fighting started, apart from those who loved a good brawl. Numerous contemporary newspaper and court reports tell of the raucousness of life in central Cardiff and Butetown pubs. One street, Charlotte Street, was demolished near the Hayes Bridge as it was impossible to police. (See Chapter 11).

The police stations were lit with gas, oil, or paraffin lamps. For most residences it was the oil lamp. This led to numerous fires, especially late at night when the alcohol in many of the lodgers' rooms led to accidents when they came home after a night out.

The late-1800s saw the building of many police stations: Clifton Street, Crwys Road, Grangetown, Canton, and Llandaff. Time stood still in various stations but none more so than Bute Street. Bute Street Police Station never caught up with mod cons, never had central heating, unlike Clifton Street, which eventually did. It is said that the roll-top desk in the sergeant's office in 1965 and the large enquiry desk table were the originals from its opening in 1895.

MORGUES AND INQUESTS

There was a morgue built into the rear of Bute Street station as there was in Janet Street Police Station as well. Police officers from the 1890s would have used the morgue as the first port of call when bringing in dead bodies to be examined. It would be a local doctor, such as Dr Buist in Grangetown, who was called in to attend to these bodies. He also did post-mortem examinations, and was therefore a regular in magistrates courts giving evidence.

In 1895, once a body had been discovered, things moved quickly. There were no refrigerators so they had to preserve the dignity of the deceased person as well as they could. In many of the morgues there were no windows so they relied on the thickness of the walls to keep the room cool.

An officer would contact the coroner to arrange an inquest, which might be held upstairs in a public house. Once the public room had been found, the police officer would inform the coroner who would organise a gathering of local people to act as a jury. The police officer would arrange, along with administration colleagues to have the handwritten statements ready for the court's perusal.

The Docklands Morgue was located at the rear of Bute Street Police Station. (where the sliding double doors are in this photo)

Cardiff City police constables attending inquests or the coroner's courts in later years would have seen a major difference in the venues. The majority of inquests in the mid-19th century were held in public houses, usually the nearest to the event. Many of the larger Bute Street pubs that had meeting *and* committee rooms would be hired out regularly for inquests. It must have been convenient for the parties involved to have a drink after experiencing the realities of court life. One wonders, once the coroner had departed the premises, whether a good time was had by all, including the local officers.

Inquests were held in many pubs in and around Cardiff. The Three Elms Public House in Whitchurch was also used on a regular basis by the coroner. At the end of the 19th century it was used to decide what happened to a man who had been killed very near the pub! He had loaded a cart of boulders from a quarry. His horse bolted and a wheel on the wagon drove over his abdomen as he lay on the ground. He was dead within half an hour.

As the century wore on, the more serious coroner's inquests were held in the police courts across the town. By the end of the 19th century it seems the practice of pub inquests had died out completely.

Inquests were held almost immediately after the body was found, and in most cases the next day. If a death involved a murder, manslaughter, or even natural causes, and the witnesses were from a ship it was imperative to get on with the process as quickly as possible. Sailors departed for every corner of the earth and were highly unlikely ever to return, so justice had to be swift.

In 1965 morgues attached to police stations were a memory, but the rooms remained part of the fabric of the building in some stations. Curran Road was the main city morgue, but was usurped by St Davids Hospital and Cardiff Royal Infirmary morgues. The system had become much more efficient with dedicated coroner's officers and courts, and manned by police officers.

Jones Court, 2017 A restored Victorian residential row, once used as a coroner's court

STATION LIFE

Throughout the history of the police force, busy and well-manned police stations in nearly all the Cardiff suburbs became a centre for local life. In the event of any kind of trouble it was easy to send a runner to the station to tell the desk officer. Queues formed quickly when people arrived to visit relatives in the cells, to report accidents, special watches on their premises (a property that required additional policing for a short period), or produce their driving documents in later years.

Police officers in both 1895 and 1965 were to be found in side rooms writing out statements from witnesses in long hand for submission to the courts. Typewriters were in evidence in the 1960s, with reams of carbon paper and bottles of correction fluid littering the desks. Fax machines and copiers were unheard of as the force went lumbering into the brave new world of amalgamation with Merthyr, Swansea, and Glamorgan constabularies in 1969.

Something else that George Hinge would not have been used to (and which revolutionised the art of criminal detecting), was fingerprints. In the 1890s the use of identification via fingerprints was in its infancy. It was in South America that the method was first used successfully in the early 1890s. Europe began the system of taking fingerprints from every arrested person as the norm in the early 1900s. The methods of course became more sophisticated over the years, but George Hinge, a constable stationed at Bute Street Police Station in the 1890s, would have known of them only in the last years of his service.

Every police station has its awkward areas to patrol, areas where trouble is likely to occur, or burglaries are most likely to be committed. Some police stations have many of these districts and manpower is directed to cover them as needs arise. It's also human nature, even amongst police officers, to feel some sort of perverted pride in working the roughest area of a town or city. "They've got it easy working from that nick, look what we've got to put up with?" may be a snippet of conversation one may overhear. This even relates to specific streets.

SIEGE MENTALITY

Research also seems to reflect an 'us against them' style of policing during the particularly cruel years between 1840 and 1914 in Cardiff. There would certainly have been a siege mentality once the safe confines of the familiar police station was reached but whether that continued onto the streets is a matter for hypothesis.

Men (and it was all men) together in a police station mess room sometimes saw the world outside their walls as warfare, a war they were safe from within the station. Once outside they relied totally on the public's goodwill to assist them in difficult times.

We know that there were many more policemen on the beat in those days as reports of police whistles being heard and swiftly answered seem to show. One can imagine a police officer today only having a whistle to blow in times of trouble, his or her chances of being heard by another officer would be negligible.

EARLY DETECTIVE DEPARTMENT

The Detective Department was quite a small office within the Borough compared to the final years of the city's police force. The same detectives' names keep cropping up time and time again on the court lists in the late 1800s, e.g. Scott and Dix.

Stabbings, assaults, drunkenness, prostitution, all seemed generally to incur instant arrests. The investigatory crimes, for example, murder, burglary, needed follow-up investigation by detectives. The detective department grew over the decades with each police station getting its own detachment of men, usually a sergeant and three constables. As the years rolled on and innovations led to new techniques of crime detection separate detective squads were set up, such as Fingerprint and Photography, Fraud, and Scenes of Crime.

The early Cardiff Borough and City Police Force needed more beat officers than squad officers. Large-scale unrest in or near public houses seemed quite normal and expected, considering the scores of pubs packed into very tight central areas. A staggering 131 pubs were licensed in the compact area of Cardiff town centre in 1901 and scores more drinking dens were unlicensed.

When we examine the methods of detection available to Victorian detectives it is a miracle they were so successful. Forensics were at a very early stage, there was no DNA knowledge, no forms of document communication other than by post, no sophisticated electronic connections, albeit phones were becoming the norm from 1880 with the introduction of the first trunk lines in the United Kingdom. They did have photographic records of prisoners but of course they could not be transmitted by technology such as fax and scanners, once again it had to be by post or other manual delivery.

BEHIND CLOSED DOORS, TIME STOOD STILL

The most amazing fact when examining the two extremes of Cardiff's policing eras is how similar the method of beat policing was, it had not changed in a century. Constable George Hinge came on duty in Bute Street police station in 1890. If by magic the same man came on duty in 1965 and once he had walked into the entry foyer, George would be quite at home. Behind those historic doors time had simply stood still. Nothing had changed at all.

He would be wearing a Cardiff Police uniform, carrying just a truncheon for protection, and have a police whistle in his breast pocket, secured by a chain. The Reserve Officer (desk man) would be stoking the coal fire (there were no radiators) and sitting behind the original, giant station desk. Blotting paper would be much in prominence as would inkwells.

A large green Occurrence Book would be on the desk and one phone. The phone had no dial-out facility. On lifting the receiver an officer waited for the switchboard at the central law courts to answer.

The mess room, with its coal fire, ancient built-in lockers and wooden table were still being used.

The only difference George would come across on his journey through the ages would be upstairs. The top two floors were spacious, with high ceilings. In 1890 these floors were full of officers making their way to their rooms to crash out on the single beds in the dormitory. They were made up mostly of single men's quarters though we know by the 1950s married men were living there with their wives.

The most famous officer of the 1950s was Butetown's most fondly-remembered officer, Constable Viv Brooks, who also lived there with his wife, Jean. One fellow-officer remembers them complaining about the damp but they weren't there long, moving on to pastures new.

That practice finished in the late 1950s, and by 1965 the upper floors were in a state of total dereliction and never used again.

A 1965 officer paraded for duty in the mess room with the Sergeant preciously holding two books – the State and the Occurrence Book. Victorian Constable Hinge would recognise them both. The State was a daily book of postings: who was to work which beat and who was on a day off.

This, therefore, could be referred to in attempting to trace officers on duty in months and years gone by on certain beats. The Occurrence Book was the station bible documenting daily goings-on. For example, criminal intelligence, insecure premises, special watch, official information, and pub visits which needed follow ups, all this was passed between shifts.

BOBBIES ON BIKES

An unlikely mode of transport that has bridged the ages of Cardiff police is the bicycle. In the 1940s and 1950s officers used their own bikes, and were paid a 'bike allowance'. One 96-year-old former Cardiff police officer remembers it was half a crown paid in your wage packet. In today's money, 12½ pence.

Scroll back to 1900, when an Inspector from Bridgend heard that a Cardiff murderer was being held at Cowbridge police station and he rode his bike all the way there. He had probably worked out it was quicker than taking the train to Llantrisant, changing and then going down the single line to Cowbridge Town station. Nowadays, we see still see officers on bikes, but with crash helmets not police helmets, with protective clothing not just a tunic and a whistle.

POLICE ON FIRE DUTY

Outside Roath Police Station, police officers also doubled-up as fire officers in times of emergency.

POLICE POWERS

Acts of Parliament applied by Victorian officers on street arrests were the same ones used by officers right up until the end of the force in 1969. Both eras used Common Law and powers from the the Vagrancy Act 1824, Malicious Damage Act 1861, Offences Against the Persons Act 1861, and even exercised laws going back to the 14th century: Justice of the Peace Act 1361. One officer who joined in 1965 remembers learning these Acts word for word in training school and arresting persons for various offences under all of the acts named above. 'Hawkers and pedlars wandering abroad from town to town' were often apprehended using those exact words and cited verbatim in court.

The Cardiff courts and the style and methodology of arrests and prosecutions were the same and, bizarrely, in many cases, the fines were identical. £2 for prostitution or drunkenness was still the amount being demanded in court in the 1960's as it had been in the 1880s.

One contrasting thing a modern police officer will definitely observe is the severity of punishments. No penal servitude with hard labour, no flogging, and of course no death penalty. Inside the police station the philosophy and system might have changed very little. What *had* changed was life outside the police station, and the punishments that those who set the laws deemed appropriate.

STREET ARRESTS

Victorian and Edwardian constables usually had just one option with an arrested person: drag them fighting all the way to the police station, however far that was. If it were two or more people he was arresting, blowing his whistle *may* have brought assistance. There were horse carts or horse-drawn cabs that the offenders could have been forced into. Not every constabulary had horse-drawn prison vans and they were definitely not always available.

Compare that with today. Every officer has a personal radio to hail assistance from fellow beat officers and police vehicles on call. He or she should not wait long for assistance. On balance, there are fewer officers on the streets today to give assistance, but they do have proper protective clothing and modern information technology. Beat constables are not as prominent in our modern era as technology and different styles of policing are introduced, but they have to combat unruly street behaviour with fewer officers. This illustrates an age-old debate, what is for the public's best, pro-active or re-active policing?

The one consistent factor, whether it be 1865, 1965, or the 21st century, is people being intoxicated and fighting. Some things never change.

BLACK MARIAS

Victorian George Hinge if around in 1965 would no doubt be impressed by the modern police telephone pillars and the ability to call the one van available within twenty minutes. His was a horse-and-cart world.

It is interesting to analyse the differences in street arrests over one hundred years. An officer in 1965 who was on duty where a drunken woman was 'performing' had several transport options after the arrest. He could drag her (and that was the norm) to a police pillar and telephone for the van to be brought down. A traffic officer would leave his central office and drive to the scene in a Black Maria (this was originally an American term for a police van and pictured left).

Alternatively, he could stop a passing car, but with a fighter that was unsatisfactory. The public were vital in giving the officer assistance or at least in helping to call for assistance.

SUBSISTENCE

Meal breaks in police stations is, and was, always looked forward to, whether due to inclement weather or simply to get over a rough duty. Today an officer may bring in a Chinese takeaway, a curry, or a kebab or two. In bigger police stations there may be a canteen. There are also numerous quality cafés for refreshments to be purchased, and of course supermarkets.

In the 60s wages were low and it was breakfast that was the most eagerly looked forward to. Why? Each of the butchers on a beat officer's patch were visited on mornings prior to breakfast where liver, kidneys, chops, eggs, etc., were supplied to the hungry coppers at a very competitive price. These were transported back to the police stations, usually in the pocket of an officer's cape, then fried on gas rings using lard or fat that had been in the pan for weeks. On nights it was always sandwiches. It was the only snack available, made at home usually by 'the wife'.

One officer remembers the first proper Chinese café opening in Bute Street just after World War II. Everyone was made welcome. Prior to that, Chinese food was only available in Chinese Lodging Houses and then only for visiting Chinese nationals not usually the locals. He states a Chinese man ran the *Union Jack Café* at the top of Bute Street, later to become Ted Davies' lodging house. The *Jack* was scrupulously clean, a place where an officer could rest his weary legs and hide away from the sergeant. This would have had a familiar ring to it for Constable Hinge in his era. Prior to World War I you can imagine it was sandwiches of cheese or meats.

The common denominator through the ages in police stations is... the cuppa! One can imagine a wild and stormy night in Llandaff or Grangetown in 1895 and an officer is patrolling his beat. Could there be anything more cheering than to enter the station to be welcomed by a roaring coal fire built up in the grate and a kettle sitting alongside bubbling away. The officer's Great Coat or mac would be hung over the station's 'clothes horse' to dry whilst he took his refreshment. In 1965 in some of the older stations it was the same, the only difference being a cell had been designated as the drying room.

Pen-y-peel Road, 2017. Over a century ago, these houses were home to many of Cardiff's police officers.

Two Cardiff Borough police officers (centre left) on duty at the junction of High Street and Duke Street.

Cardiff City Police Record of Service for John Thomas, who joined in 1919. He had been wounded in the Battle of the Somme in the Great War, and was the first officer to retire after World War Two.

CARDIFF CITY POLICE.

RECORD OF SERVICE OF :— John Thomas   No. 24 C

DATE of joining	1 April 1919
" formally appointed	22 November 1922
" and place of birth	23 April 1893 at Cowbridge, Glam.
Previous occupation	Labourer and Soldier
Former Public Service—Police	Nil.
" " Army, Navy	10½ years. Army. 3rd Royal Sussex Regt.
Married or Single	Single
Height	5' 11½"
Qualified "First Aid"	Certificate 8.8.1920 Life Saving August 1921.

PAY AND ADVANCEMENTS.

Joined	38/-	1 April	1919
Desborough Scale	70/-	11 April	1919
Advanced	74/-	21 August	1921
Advanced	76/-	1st April	1922
Advanced	78/-	1 April	1923
Advanced	88/-	1 April	1924
Advanced	82/-	1 April	1925
Advanced	84/-	1 April	1926
Advanced	86/-	1 April	1927
Advanced	88/-	1 April	1928
Advanced	90/-	1 April	1929
Advanced	92/6	9th April	1936
Advanced	95/-	9th May	1941
CO 6 of 9/41	—	Reg. 59	
New Scale	123/-	1st April	1945
1-9-44 War Supplement of 19/- per pensionable			
22-12-44 " " -23/- per			

Retired on the 18th May 1945 on a pension of £213.18.8 per annum.

Certificate of Service issued on 18th May 1945. — "During the period of his service his conduct was

Exemplary

[signature]
Chief Constable.

Received :— Certificate of Service
Birth Certificate   J. Thomas
Certificate of Demobilisation   1/6/45

ATTACHMENT, TRANSFERS, SUSPENSIONS.

Transferred "C" to "C"   25th April 1944

CHAPTER TWO

Street life

> ROBBERIES, &c., IN CARDIFF.
>
> ROBBERY.—On Saturday night a sailor was robbed of 11s. 6d. in a house of ill-fame, 31, Charlotte-street.
>
> ANOTHER SIMPLETON.—On Tuesday night a foreign sailor, belonging to the barque Margarette, went with a girl to a house of ill fame in Charlotte-street, where he was robbed of £1 16s.

A typical newspaper report. Victims were not always treated sympathetically.

THE MOST VIOLENT STREET IN CARDIFF

Local Cardiff newspapers in the 1880s ran a competition to find the most violent and troublesome street in Cardiff. Reporters followed constables to report on the troubles they encountered. Others looked at the court lists and made notes of the addresses of the arrested persons. It appeared that the distinction for the roughest street was a race between Mary Ann Street and Charlotte Street. Both were notorious and virtually every house had at some time been the subject of criminal or disorderly behaviour. The majority of the residents in the streets were licensed lodging-house keepers so they attracted a motley assortment of passing trade. Most houses supplied beer and sported names such as the *Parrot Tavern, Nicholls Arms, Operative Tavern, Butchers Arms, Cork and Waterford,* and the *Flying Eagle.* If the houses were unlicensed they probably still sold beer and were often more cause of trouble than the licensed establishments.

There is an irony to think of those journalists following Victorian officers to get the best stories from the front line and campare it with today's 24-hour news gatherers doing virtually the same thing. Some things never change.

WORKING GIRLS

If you were wandering up Bute Street in 1965 from the police station you'd encounter many of the prostitutes who worked the area. Nothing much had changed from the old days except perhaps there were fewer 'working girls'. Those of the 1960s were making money, a few drank, but compared to the Victorian prostitutes they were a mild bunch, (perhaps with one or two exceptions!). Victorian street women escaped from their lifestyle in drink, while propping up their drinking habit with prostitution: a vicous circle.

THE CATHAYS INCIDENT

Cathays Police Station is still operational and mostly unaltered from the days of its construction. Today it appears a quiet monument to more tumultuous times gone by, yet still serves as a useful social purpose.

In the 1890s when the area was teeming with street life and misinformed gossip on the street spread like wildfire, an incident occurred that showed how fragile public order had become. Simple suspicion, exaggerated rumours, and downright lies, gave the police a mob to sort out.

It was April, 1888, and rumours started to reach the officers of dire crimes having been committed. The officer on desk duty heard sounds outside the station window and on looking out saw a small crowd gathering. He went to the front door and was bombarded with shouts and cries of "Murder!". He closed the door, went back inside and told another officer to go out via the back door, through the yard and to the front to see what was going on. The second officer learned that the crowd had heard an awful crime of the murder of three tiny children that had taken place, and that the murderer was being held and protected inside the police station. He told the crowd there was no-one inside the cells and he had not heard anything of the incident. This initial report concerned a man who had enticed little girls into the cellar of the Wesleyan Chapel at the end of Fanny Street.

The crowd moved away from the police station, but did not entirely disperse, and rumours of the crimes became more widespread. Officers made enquiries themselves working on the adage, "There is no smoke without fire". Then someone ran into one of the crowds and shouted that a Governess in nearby Letty Street had been raped and the man was on the loose. The crowds swelled and so did the rumours. It was then said that one of the children had his

Crwys Road Board School

head severed from his body. The situation was getting nasty and out of control.

The cellar of the chapel appeared to be locked. Imagine the surprise of the caretaker, Bill Jones, when he came to the chapel to find a huge crowd surrounding the building and the police from Cathays holding them back. He made his way through the crowd, opened the cellar door and found... nothing! The police officers had to find out what was going on. The crowd would not go and was swelling in numbers.

One officer was advised to go to Letty Street and enquire at numbers 17 and 19. The residents explained that at 9.00am that day four children from the houses, all cousins, had gone to the Board School in nearby Crwys Road. One was five years of age and the others only three. It is hard to believe, but it was said that two of the three-year-olds left at noon to walk home. The older child should have been with them, but told their parents the tiny children had just wandered off. It seems not much was done at the time other than wait for them to return home. The police commenced a search but not before the rumours of the children's demise had worked up the crowd.

It was around 8.30pm that the children were found in Metal Street, Roath. They were taken to Clifton Street police station and ultimately reunited with their worried parents. One wonders if an unfortunate, innocent individual had been targeted by the mob what might have happened.

It was in 1888 that a mob had thought that Jack the Ripper was in Butetown and had targeted an innocent man. He was badly beaten as a result. It was a police constable who saved him then.

This was an era when crowds regularly surrounded police stations when a murder suspect was in custody. The police at Cathays must have been relieved as much as the parents when the little children were found. Rumours about the children missing were factual, the ensuing gossip was not. It was a lesson on the dark side of human nature and mob culture. That type of incident was a sign of the times not reflected in the final years of the Cardiff City Police.

DOWN AND OUTS

Continue your walk up Bute Street in the 60s and you may look down at the old canal bank. There you would probably see fires burning with men huddled around them. You may also see some of the men drinking purple liquid from a glass bottle. The men would probably be paralytically drunk and not in control of any of their bodily functions. Some men would just shake in a demented and uncontrollable way, some would lie prostrate and hopelessly drunk, while others just wander around mumbling indistinguishably. What is consistent with them all is, they have been drinking methylated spirits.

Many of the 'down and outs' – homeless people escaping from their awful lifestyle – drank from morning to night. You may see them lurking around during the day, carrying their bottles, sitting on doorsteps, or lying in the gutters. These sad men, many war veterans, were at the savage end of a cruel century for the homeless in Cardiff. Each one of those men had a story to tell, a story that may put our own life stories into perspective. Their stories cannot be told, none appear to be documented, which in many ways is sad. The stories that *are* documented are usually of the rich and their achievements and their philanthropic exploits, or the poor and their criminal trials.

ARRESTS OF VAGRANTS

The policing of 'unfortunates' (as they were once officially known) was a curse. It was a farcical situation for any police officer to come across, whatever the era they lived in. If it was the 1960s an officer knew that to take an 'unfortunate' person into custody for being drunk, was a pointless exercise. It was usually undertaken for the safety of the individual or the public, for example if the person was staggering into the road, therefore causing danger.

In Victorian or Edwardian times it was more harsh. There were a good many more unfortunates on the streets and those streets were densely populated. The magistrates usually fined them a paltry amount, knowing they could not pay, and sent them back on the streets to be apprehended again. Some went to prison, but there was the same result on release, back on the streets.

The problem of persistent drunken behaviour spanned the centuries and the methodology of dealing with them seemed to change very little. What has changed is what little homelessness and sleeping on the streets there is today by comparison to years ago and it is not usually accompanied by drunken and violent behaviour, at least not to the extent it did before. There are those who would argue that homelessness in the 21st century is a curse and still a major problem. Yes it is, but there can be no comparison to Victorian and Edwardian times, when homelessness was an accepted part of street life.

Some officers in all eras administered instant justice to drunken troublemakers. It usually involved getting them out of the way and down some back lane and advising them that their conduct was unacceptable. They were then left to sleep it off.

On busy nights, for example, in the St Mary Street / Caroline Street area, you wanted every uniform you could get as a show of force, and to deal with large scuffles and boisterous activity. In short, the Sergeant did not want to lose an officer for an hour or two at the most important times dealing with the comparatively harmless down and outs. The Charge Sergeant in any police station did not welcome vermin covered, unruly drunks being brought in. They were trouble, not only to fellow prisoners but also to the police officers themselves.

PUBS AND DEMOLITION

A 1960s officer experienced the end of an epoch in Cardiff. The central and Butetown areas were wiped off the face of the earth, especially the residential sections. There are few clues today as to the thriving, raucous, and ever-changing communities. What was wiped away by modernisation was not only the physical but also the internal representations of Cardiff's violent past. When researching the awful deprivation in Victorian times in areas such as Butetown, Newtown, Temperancetown, and around Bute Terrace, it was illuminating to have actually walked those same streets as many did only half a century ago . It was also the age of rampant demolition, nothing seemed to be too big, historic, or sentimental to evade the wrecking-ball frenzy.

One officer remembers going to a fight in the *Glastonbury Arms* at the top of Bute Street in the mid-60s. There, six men were fighting and he managed to gather them up and shoo them out of the front door and into the street. One man kept trying to barge his way back in and was prevented from doing so and told to go on his way.

His persistence finally succeeded when the officer asked him, "What's wrong with you? Why don't you go home?"

"I *am* home," he replied. "I'm the bloody landlord!"

An officer would have wandered through public houses that had once been at the centre of Cardiff's violent past. To research and talk about the cruel streets of Victorian Cardiff is not just based on imagination, it is based on living memory. Many of the most infamous Victorian pubs were still there in the 1960s, but some had vanished decades before.

Pubs such as *The Cornish Mount, The Tredegar* (in Bute Terrace), *The Crichton, The Loudoun, The Freemasons, The George, The West Dock, The Rothesay Castle, The Irish Club, The Cambridge, The Moulders,* and *The Peel* were still up and running, as were scores more from Victorian times. The 60s officer would have walked in them all, felt the ambience, perhaps visited the private quarters. These were pubs that would be the scenes of murder, gang violence, or places where sailors and prostitutes congregated, sung, danced, and fought. Patrons today surely know little or nothing of the long and rich past that each and every old establishment has to tell.

The 1965 officer would have walked along Bute Street, passing the same houses that were infamous half a century or so before with the bawdy activities of visiting sailors. There was probably not a yard on this street that had not hosted a violent altercation, or even a murder.

Such is the power of modern-day internet research to uncover these deeds, but of course the researcher is missing out on one thing – first-hand experience. In the central area, beat officers in the swinging 60s walked through *The Salutation, The Lifeboat, The Fishguard, The Tredegar, The Taff Vale, The Eagle, The Rhymney, The Sandon, The Vulcan, The Hope Hotel, The British Volunteer, The Greyhound, The Queens Head,* and many others. These pubs too would gain notoriety when their histories were known, and the incidents within came to light. Mary Ann Street was still standing, as were many other streets that were violent honeypots in bygone times, such as Barracks Lane, Union Street, Ruperra Street, Bute Terrace, Whitmore Lane, and School Street.

It is with the new technology adding to the ease of researching that allows us to explore and uncover the social status of public houses in Cardiff's past.

The author, in younger days, enjoying an off-duty pint in The Hope Hotel *on North Road.*

LODGING HOUSES

The lodging houses of the 1960s were pale shadows of their counterparts in the 1880s with the decline of shipping. Greek, Spanish, Chinese, Italian, and general lodgings were scattered across the whole of the Butetown area, with around 220 of them at their peak. Each brought their own particular policing problems.

Lodging houses were commonplace too in Homfray Street, Tredegar Street, Stanley Street, and Mary Ann Street. Many a fracas and subsequent arrest came from lodging houses. The reason for this being the transitory nature of the guests – many of them sailors from around the world. Add the complications of many foreign languages, mixed with alcohol, and you have a recipe for anarchy at times.

WANDER TO NEWTOWN

An officer from 1965 may wander across to Newtown and chat to the wonderful people who inhabited the area, mostly of Irish origin. None behaved like they had one hundred years previously, when raging poverty drove many of the residents to alcohol abuse and crime. *The Crichton* and *The Cambridge* pubs still stood and sold good beer to the locals, but the *Duke of Edinburgh* had closed, as had the the *Lakes of Killarney*, even though the buildings they occupied remained.

One woman, the last to leave Newtown after demolition contractors took over, used to say, "If only these streets could talk, then you'd hear some stories." All old streets have stories to tell but Newtown's stories would be much more powerful as it was a community separated from all others and a world on its own. This area was mostly inhabited by Irish immigrants escaping poverty in their home country, not knowing the lifestyle in their new home could be just as tough, or tougher.

THE LAST STOWAWAY ARREST

In the 1960s, shipping into Cardiff was negligible compared to what it once was, but still busy enough to give docks' officers tight deadlines if it was a sailor who had been arrested.

One officer came on duty in 1966 at Bute Street police station at 6.00am and told to go immediately to the central cells complex. There he was introduced to a man who had stowed away on a *Blue Star* freighter. He was found at sea hidden in the tarpaulins of a lifeboat. He was instructed by the captain to work by day and locked in the ship's brig at night.

When the ship docked at Cardiff the police were called and, for some undocumented reason, the British Transport Police could not deal with him and the City Police lent a hand. The officer remembers typing out by hand a charge sheet, in triplicate, with the offence reading 'stowing away' He charged the man, and was present in the Magistrates Court when he appeared in front of the Stipendiary Magistrate.

After the accused man had pleaded guilty, the officer, Constable 230A, gave his evidence and a summary of the circumstances. In the court was the captain and some of the ship's crew. The captain had informed the officer that he was willing to take the man back on board and he could work his passage. It seemed a rather pleasant affair all round. The Stipendiary saw that the maximum sentence he could give was one month. He actually sentenced him to just one day, which he had already served, so he was released at once into the custody of the captain. In the company of the police officer he was returned to the ship. There, he was locked in the brig and the captain instructed that he was not to be released from custody until the ship had cleared the main dock gates and was in the Bristol Channel.

All so simple for the 60s officer, but a very rare occurrence. It would have been a daily part of a docks officer's duty in those heady days of Victorian Cardiff's hustle and bustle.

THE DETECTIVE DEPARTMENT'S LAST DAYS

It was a mandate in the Cardiff City Police, even up to its demise in 1969, for every crime to be visited by a Detective or a Scenes of Crime Officer. The intelligence gathered via crime visits was invaluable and added to the knowledge of a detective's home patch. It also reassured the public, and in many cases led to the crime being cleared up.

Modus operandi was a very important part of a detective's arsenal. He knew his patch and everyone in it. The main methods of detection were conversation, knowledge, and enthusiasm based on a total concentration to his dedicated area.

Detectives in the 1950s, 60s, and much of the 70s, used laborious, but efficient, card systems to record persons of interest, their records, and their current status, e.g. wanted or missing. Their known address(es), associates, and family were all catalogued.

Wanted persons were nationally circulated via a *Police Gazette* which was reported, usually weekly, to all forces, complete with the name, address, and photographs of wanted and missing persons. On receipt of the gazette at the various local criminal records offices, an officer would disseminate the information and update the force's card system. Cancellations i.e. arrests of wanted persons, were also circulated via this methodology.

Later, they became area circulations being put together via the criminal records offices in a more localised way, e.g. the Western Criminal Record Office which covered the South Wales region.

THE LAST BLACK AND WHITE MUGSHOTS

In the 1960s, Cardiff City Police had a fingerprint and photograph room in the central police station cells. All arrested persons had to be taken there and processed.

Perhaps George Hinge may have recognised the camera! In 1968 it was still an ancient plate camera complete with a black, cloth cover. The cells man would insert the large slide in the back of the camera, pull out a sheet, take the picture using a long wire attached to the shutter with a button-push at the other end. Then pop the sheet back into the plate. The slides were collected every morning by the photography department. The resulting pictures were, of course in black and white. This, one would imagine, was exactly the same system as in the 1890s.

It's fascinating to view the arrest records of the 19th century – to see the faces of those who were in the eye of the law. These records held all the pertinent details an officer needed to know about a suspect or a convicted criminal.

AND FINALLY...

Aggression, greed, drunkenness, and sexual offences are a part of human nature, whatever the era, and a modern officer has the same basic human failings to deal with. Today, however, he or she is watched more than at any other time in history. CCTV, mobile phones, and 24-hour news, means someone, somewhere is always watching.

They may have the crime-fighting and safety technology, but they haven't got the same freedom to make mistakes or deal with street offences in their own way. Some of the old ways were often with the wholehearted approval of the public.

Constable Hinge with a taser in 1890s Tiger Bay. Now there's something for the imagination!

CHAPTER THREE

Ripper victim: the murder of Mary Jane Kelly

*Mary Ann Street, between Bute Terrace and Bridge Street, 1977.
Did Jack the Ripper's last victim walk this pavement?
Yes, if you believe the victim herself, but can you believe her?
It has puzzled researchers for over a century.*

Mary Jane Kelly was said to be buxom and attractive with auburn hair. She was nicknamed, 'Ginger', 'Fair Emma', and 'Black Mary', which seems to point to various periods of her life and hairstyle. It is said by Ripper researchers that Mary Jane Kelly was born in Limerick on 25th August, 1863, but that cannot be verified. She did move to Wales when she was a young girl. She told friends she had up to seven brothers and one sister. There is no definitive evidence to support that either. It was some time during the mid to late 1860s when her journey was made, alongside thousands of other Irish people, in an attempt to escape poverty and in hope of a new life in another country.

Mary's father found work as a gaffer (a middle-man between the workers and management in an ironworks), either in Caernarfonshire or Carmarthenshire.

If it was Caernarfonshire it would be a pretty fair bet that John Kelly went to work at the De Winton's Foundry in Caernarfon. Why? Limerick had a main thoroughfare to Dublin and at that time there were ships to take emigrants to various places including North Wales, which was close. The ironworks had been started in the 1840s then expanded in the 1860s. It grew to employ around 250 men. It was a thriving business in heavy engineering, turning out steam locomotives, agricultural machinery, industrial plant, and many other iron products. The main building still stands there today. If Kelly had worked in Caernarfon it would have been a long haul to get to South Wales where his 16-year-old daughter, Mary Jane, was to meet Davies, her husband. The 150-mile drive to the South Wales valleys, the location of the coal mines, today takes around three to four hours by car, so it would have been a trip of several days by horse and cart, or on foot.

Therefore, perhaps it was Carmarthenshire instead, not Caernarfonshire, where he ended up. There were several foundries in the area, and lies in the south west of Wales. There were also ferries and sailing ships from the south east of Ireland to this part of Wales.

Mary Jane Kelly told her friends that she found her way to Glamorgan, which was at that time populated by hundreds of coal mines and iron foundries, and was no doubt where her father John would have found work. Was it in Glamorgan where father and daughter parted company? Fatalities in industrial South Wales were commonplace and perhaps John Kelly was one of those dismal statistics. We shall never know as the trail of evidence has long-since gone cold.

In Glamorgan, at the age of around 16 years, Mary Jane met a coal miner called Davies, whom she married. It is not known whether she had children by him, but she probably did. She stated to friends that he had been killed in an explosion and afterwards she moved to Cardiff. It was a bad move as ultimately what she learnt in Cardiff led to her death. The facts of Mary's life in Wales are only known via her own version of events as told to friends in London, and her movements are not provable, as there are no corroborating records of either her parents, or her marital status.

If there is something complicated or hurtful in one's past it is easier to give the briefest of information in order to keep it quiet. Many prostitutes had aliases, not wanting knowledge of their profession to get back to family members.

It is not known why, how, or even if, she gravitated to Cardiff but one can surmise that Cardiff was an attractive destination as it was the centre of several Irish communities set up between the 1830s and 1870s. She would have been welcomed here. Research shows the Irish people were very hospitable at the time to their own and to anyone down on their luck, which obviously Mary was. She could lose herself in the scores of Irish-run pubs and meeting houses in the centre of Cardiff. The problem was the communities were impoverished, and to such a degree that many women did anything to obtain money simply to exist. Of course, they saw their major asset as their own body and this led to hundreds of women becoming prostitutes in the busy sea port. This miserable life also led to escapism through alcohol.

It is said by her contemporaries that Mary took to the streets in Cardiff and therefore it follows, if true, that she was probably often drunk. Witnesses in later court hearings stated Mary was a quiet and rather reserved woman, when not in drink. It would appear also that she was an attractive woman and sought after by men willing to pay.

The back streets of Tiger Bay and Bute Terrace were bustling as the port grew. Public houses and their girls drew sailors in after long passages at sea. They had money to spend and most of it went on drink and fun. Perhaps the most notorious of these pubs was the *Flying Eagle* in Charlotte Street, which is further documented in this book. (see Chapter 11)

There are other stories relating to Mary Jane Kelly and her residence in Cardiff during the 1880s that are a little harder to investigate. She told one London friend that she spent eight months in an infirmary in Cardiff. This could have been correct as there was a thriving and well-used infirmary near the Irish residential areas. The problem is that no-one knows if she meant working or as an in-patient, or if it was true at all. There are other unverified stories, that Mary was in an infirmary in London with venereal disease.

Working girls made friends amongst themselves. Theirs was a tough and dangerous existence and they relied on each other for protection. They also frequented the rough sailors' pubs, where a pick-up was made, followed by a short walk to a local house or lane for sex, then back to the pub. It is not known whether Mary accepted her way of life, enjoyed it, or hated it, but what we do know is that she chased the bright lights and bigger money. One day in the early 1880s (it's impossible to tell from records exactly when) Mary caught a train from Cardiff General Station for London. She would never return.

Mary Jane Kelly became the fifth and final victim of Jack the Ripper on the 9th November, 1888. Her awful death is well-documented and subject even today to exacting analysis.

One witness into the investigation of Mary's murder stated that as he saw her going back to her rooms with a man, she was singing loudly *A Violet From Mother's Grave*, a music hall favourite of the time. By this time, she claimed to have visited Paris and renamed herself, Marie Jeanette Kelly, the name that is inscribed on her gravestone in St Patrick's R.C. Cemetery, Leightonstone, London. But, is it her true place of burial? The exact location is not known.

One can imagine the *Green Fields of Erin* public house in Mary Ann Street Cardiff one evening in 1880s. On one stool sits Minnie Maguire and on another Mary Jane Kelly. The drinking has started and they both stand up, pint glasses in hand singing. Locals and sailors alike clap and cheer, plying the girls with more drink. This was the way of life for many impoverished women.

The only indisputable fact in the narrative above is Mary Jane Kelly was murdered on the 9th November, 1888. It was gruesome. Her nose and ears were slashed off, her face disfigured so badly she was unrecognisable. Most of Mary Jane Kelly's internal organs had been removed and placed on a table. A poignant addition to the awful sight was that her clothes were arranged neatly on a chair. This perhaps was as a result not of Jack the Ripper, but of Mary herself as she folded her clothes before getting into bed.

None of the information she had supplied to friends about her past life is verifiable. Perhaps she was not a Kelly at all. It could have been a name she made up when she arrived in London. Perhaps she had not been brought up in Wales, perhaps she had not married, perhaps she had never even been to Cardiff. The 'facts' that are so often re-told in books about her life were the tales told to lovers and friends in London. None is verifiable, they could be true in whole or part, or entirely fictional. Mary may have ended up in a Catholic cemetery, but she may have been protestant.

Mary Jane Kelly is an enigma, her life story a conundrum that many have tried to solve. All have failed. Some researchers have trawled hospital records, and birth records in Limerick, or searched out for the alleged family members, but it has all come to nothing. A search of records to date has found no mention of a woman of that name or nickname in any Cardiff police court in the late 1800s, which seems remarkable for a known prostitute in the area.

If we followed Incident Room methodology in an attempt to solve the mystery we would ask questions:

Question:- Was Mary Jane Kelly her real name?

Question:- If not, what was her name?

Question:- Was she from Limerick?

Question:- Did she leave Ireland and travel to Wales?

Question:- Did her life's path really include Wales?

Question:- When she arrived in London was that the time that she assumed the name Mary Jane Kelly?

Without provable evidence, all the police had at the time was a body.

There have been many people who have tried to answer the above questions by travelling to specific locations or following 'clue trails'. However, there's no trace, no definitive evidence, no luck.

Another obvious question is, "Why tell everyone she spent most of her life in Wales?" Was it simply a cover, or was it based on fact? She certainly knew the names Caernarfonshire or Carmarthenshire. The witnesses were not sure which county name she had used, it was one or the other. So far as can be discerned no-one by the name of John Kelly, with a background to match, has been found working in an ironworks, but that is so far. He could have worked in his real name, which may not have been Kelly, assuming Mary had invented Kelly.

Mary had told a friend she worked as a cleaner in the Infirmary in Cardiff. Had her name been entered into records? No Mary Jane Kelly is listed.

If she was born in Ireland, which probably was the case, then the nearest port of entry into mainland Britain would be a Welsh one. There were numerous in those days, even small Welsh seaside villages boasted regular Irish links, one being Aberdovey. Now silted up, in mid-Victorian times this was a thriving shipping port with vessels going back and fore to Ireland, including Cork. The same could be said for Cardigan in West Wales. The River Teifi in Mary Kelly's days was navigable. Now that river too is silted up.

Without teams of detectives any theory is based on wishful thinking or opinion, not fact. The flimsy evidence points to a young woman leaving a life of poverty in Ireland and crossing into Wales, which is a likely scenario. To guess what followed is a leap into the dark, but there is a probability that she made her way to Cardiff. Why would she tell people she 'became bad' in Cardiff and learnt the ways of prostitution? Cardiff at that time was a real hot spot for pubs, prostitution, drunkenness and violence. The concentrated slum residential areas of the docklands and centre were a lure to thousands of foreign sailors coming in to load the 'black gold', coal.

Whatever her name was, the final piece of her life's jigsaw was the move to London. Cardiff at that time did have a train service to the English capital. So, it seems the two ends of her life's story can be accepted: born in Ireland, died in London. What happened in-between is anybody's guess.

Ripper victim, Mary Jane Kelly's, grave, or is it? In the name of Marie Jeanette Kelly, as she changed her name following a trip to France.

When her body was found, mutilated beyond recognition, carved up by a lunatic, her inner parts spread about the room, the truth of her real identity died with her. Mary Jane Kelly lies in St Patrick's Roman Catholic cemetery, Leytonstone, London. Her gravestone bears the name Marie Jeanette Kelly.

The very name of Jack the Ripper has gone into folklore, even raising him to the status of some romantic anti-hero. He was not! He was a vile woman-hater who practised the most sadistic rituals on women to feed his own personal hang-ups. An ugly and dreadful individual.

Whilst turning over page after page of the Cardiff Borough Police charge books of the 1870s and 80s in the archive, and then viewing the endless thumbnail black and white photographs of offenders, one wonders if one of those faces staring out is a woman who later called herself Mary Jane Kelly. We shall never know. To use a line from the TV show, *X-Files*: 'The truth is out there.'

The words to the song are nostalgic and emotive. It appears to have been her favourite song, the song she was singing as she walked to her demise alongside Jack the Ripper.

A Violet from Mother's Grave

Scenes of my childhood arise before my gaze,
Bringing recollections of bygone happy days,
When down in the meadow in childhood I would roam;
No one's left to cheer me now within that good old home.
Father and mother they have passed away.
Sister and brother now lay beneath the clay;
But while life does remain, to cheer me I'll retain
This small violet I plucked from mother's grave.

Chorus

Only a violet I plucked when but a girl,
And oft' times when I'm sad at heart, this flow'r has given me joy,
But while life does remain, in memoriam I'll retain
This small violet I plucked from mother's grave.

Well I remember my dear old mother's smile,
As she used to greet me when I returned from toil;
Always knitting in the old arm chair,
Father used to sit and read for all us children there.
But now all is silent around the good old home,
They all have left me in sorrow here to roam;
While life does remain, in memoriam I'll retain
This small violet I plucked from mother's grave.

CHAPTER FOUR

'The dreadful Canton husband murder'

As an investigating detective, to come across a witness who states something so startling and of such evidential value in a murder case, is an unimaginable bonus. This is what one female witness revealed to detectives about a woman suspected of murder. The suspect had come up to the witness in the street and said, "Yes, I have come out [of prison], my girl. It will not be for two months, nor six months – next time, it will be the rope." The woman just released from prison was Mary-Ann Phillips. The year was 1887. This is her story.

Mary-Ann Phillips lived in Pembroke Road, Canton with her husband, William. His age is a subject of debate, but put between 70 and 80 years of age. They had been married for around fifteen years.

William's brother, John, had owned properties in the notorious Charlotte Street. These he left to William in his will after his death. William's sister kept *The Castle Inn* in Frederick Street and he lived with her prior to his marriage to Mary-Ann. He followed his sister when she became landlady of *The Horse and Groom* in Womanby Street. There, he met Mary-Ann and they married –

living in various houses in Dinas Powis, Ely Road, and Ethel Street prior to moving to Pembroke Street. William also had an interest in the *Marquis of Bute* public house. William made a will and left it all to his wife except the cash from one house in Charlotte Street, which he left to his nieces.

Womanby Street, with Cardiff Castle clock tower in the background. The Horse and Groom pub (on the left with fixed lantern), where William met his first wife, Mary-Ann..

William and Mary-Ann did not get on and she, being more mobile than her frail husband, ruled the roost. She was aggressive towards him. It was she though who had to fetch the coal, set the fires, and warm the house for him, but it was a job she often failed to undertake. It appears she was physically violent towards him, perhaps, but only perhaps, in retribution to aggression shown towards her in her past. Who knows? It is certain that the old man was not in any state to show much aggression in return, or defend himself.

Pembroke Road, 2017.

Whatever happened inside the Pembroke Road house, one thing is for sure, William Phillips on the 28th June managed to call a police officer to the house and he took out a summons against his wife for assault. This resulted in a court case leading to Mary being bound over to keep the peace, (and therefore not assault her husband), for six months. Being bound over required a surety or a bond, which she failed to provide so Mary-Ann stayed in prison for the whole six months. It can only be imagined that William struggled to survive without daily assistance other than from neighbours or family.

On the 27th December, 1887 Mary-Ann was released and returned to live with her husband. Imagine William's thoughts when he heard the key turning in the door lock and there was Mary, home again.

A number of people living in the street were used to a commotion emanating from the house. Several had seen the woman in the past chasing her husband around the garden area and street with a broom and hitting him when she caught up with him. One had seen him on his knees pleading for mercy as she waved the broom above him. His cries did not work, she struck him hard with the brush. He had managed to crawl away with Mary striking him the brush until he got inside the house.

William must either have been a cantankerous, wicked old man or Mary-Ann a virago of a woman, or perhaps a combination of both. It is a close neighbour who can clear it up for us.

Margaret Thomas's father was William's uncle so she knew him well. On the 29th December, Mary-Ann Phillips brought her elderly husband to Margaret's nearby house and demanded back some bedclothes that she alleged William had given them whilst she was in prison. She had brought her husband with her to face Margaret. Her husband had denied giving his relative the bedclothes whereupon Margaret heard Mary-Ann say to William,

"You old vagabond, where have you taken the clothes?"

William replied "Hush my dear."

She again verbally abused him and started shaking her fist in his face. Then she struck him with her fist and knocked him down into a chair. So the scenario, as observed by another witness, Elizabeth Thomas, was of a frail, timid old man and a violent, nasty woman.

Also on the 29th December, she had a conversation with a friend Catherine Andrews, who, meeting her in the street, said, "You have come out, Mrs Phillips; take care you don't get into trouble again."

"Yes," Mary-Ann replied, "I have come out, my girl. It will not be for two months, nor six months – next time, it will be the rope." A clear declaration of her intent.

Catherine Andrews was living at 18, Edward Street, Canton and had bumped into Mary-Ann in Glamorgan Street. Catherine then saw the old man making his way up Glamorgan Street towards them.

On seeing him, Mary-Ann said, "The old devil. He was only let out of hell this morning."

As he approached them Mary-Ann went to strike him saying, "You old devil. I wish you were dead." He held up his walking stick to prevent his wife from hitting him. On doing so, she pushed him against the wall of a house. Catherine was used to seeing them fight and used to seeing Mary-Ann attacking her husband.

On the 30th December, 1887 an Annie Vulgaris went to the Phillips's home to pay her rent. Annie lived in a house owned by the old man and she had to pay each week under the usual threat of eviction. It is interesting that Mr Phillips had owned a Charlotte Street house. It was this street that vied for notoriety at the time for violence, prostitution, and robbery. The street was so notorious that it was later demolished in an attempt to clear the area of the trouble.

Mr Phillips owned many properties. When Annie went into the Phillips' home to pay the rent she asked where the old man was. Mary-Ann Phillips told her he was upstairs unwell.

She said "If he wasn't unwell I would get up there and throw him down!" She also told Annie Vulgaris that whilst she was in prison her husband had been collecting the rents and refused to tell her where he put the money.

One rather nasty comment she uttered to Annie Vulgaris was, "He's had £25 from Mr Grosvenor. If he doesn't tell me where it is I'll pull his liver through my teeth!"

She further let it be known to Annie that some of her husband's relatives had been visiting their home and stolen a number of items, including their marriage certificate. Mary-Ann was in a bad mood and ran upstairs where Annie heard her shout at her husband, "Did you sleep with your niece?"

He replied "No, my dear."

Another of the Phillips's neighbours in Pembroke Road was Mary Ann McDougall and her husband. The houses are constructed so the scullery, the main food storage room, are adjacent to each other. Therefore, the noises from one scullery could be heard next door.

It was 8.00am on the last day of the year, 31st December, 1887 when she first heard the cries of William Phillips. She seemed well-acquainted with his pleading for mercy. McDougall heard the sound of punches and his reactions, as he was obviously hurt. It is astounding that the McDougalls did nothing about it. Either they were so used to it, or getting involved was not something that was done, or was unwise to do.

Witnesses stated that they heard Mary-Ann screaming at her husband accusing him of sleeping with his niece and prostitutes whilst she was doing her six months remand on breach of the peace charges.

The disturbance seemed to go on all morning. Mrs McDougall stated that at around lunchtime she heard the old man shouting, "Murder! Murder!" She heard Mary-Ann Phillips screaming at her husband, obviously striking him, and his pleading for mercy.

McDougall could not understand the majority of Mary-Ann's shouting as it was in the Welsh language but it was obvious what was going on. It was around 1.00pm that the cries and screaming ceased. Still, the neighbour did nothing, neither calling the police nor knocking the door to see what had happened. It was left probably as just another day in the life.

McDougall said she next saw Mary-Ann at midnight on New Year's Eve. Phillips had been out and was returning to the house and was obviously under the influence of alcohol. She said that her husband had a nosebleed and she had tried to clean it up.

It was at 11.30am the following morning, 1st January, 1888 that Mary-Ann Phillips called at the nearby surgery of Dr Buist.

She was agitated. She told the doctor that her husband had fallen down the stairs and had a nose bleed. Buist knew well the old man, who he put at around 80 years of age. Indeed, he knew him well enough to describe him as frail and with hardly any physical power.

He called at the house about half an hour later and was let in by Mary-Ann. He was shown to the kitchen where he saw the body of William lying on the floor. He was deceased. It was noted that he was in a clean shirt which did not show signs of blood on it. The shirt seems to have been only half put on. Nearby, he noticed a broom with blood marks on it.

Mary-Ann told the doctor that William had fallen downstairs the previous day at around noon. This was later found to be not true as it was at this time that McDougall had heard the man being hit and punched and screaming murder. The doctor noted marks upon his hands, face, and head. On a much closer examination he saw that the left hand was seriously bruised. His face was a mass of bruising, he counted around twenty major injuries to the face and temple. His arms were riddled with bruises and there were breakages of bones above the wrist. There were fractured ribs, this being discovered on post-mortem later. In fact, the man had all the signs of a severe, frenzied, and sustained beating that had led to his death.

Police constables were called from Canton Police Station and, on seeing the deceased, they immediately informed the detective department. Inspector George Lewis attended.

Found in various locations were sheets, pillows, and various items of clothing all covered with blood. Enquiries commenced and Mary-Ann Phillips was arrested on a charge of murdering her husband William. It seemed the evidence was one of an open and shut case. It did not need much forensic or medical evidence.

While the police made enquiries, William Phillips was conveyed to the church in the Vale of Glamorgan and interred in the family vault. The funeral was made difficult, as only the horse-drawn hearse was allowed to enter the street. His family and other mourners were not allowed into Pembroke Road as the condition of the street was too slushy and unkempt.

The Assize Court sat in March 1888, the final day of the trial being the 16th, in front of Mr Justice Stephen (shown right from a court drawing). There was a lot of interest in the trial especially from women. Indeed, so much interest the ladies' benches were ticket only. One newspaper called the incident 'The Dreadful Canton Husband Murder.'

MR JUSTICE STEPHEN,

When the court opened, ladies rushed in to get the best seats with some hurrying across the prisoner's dock. There was some laughing and jibes as one of the ladies stopped in the box and pretended to be a defendant. She got short shrift from the Clerk of the Court.

Mary-Ann Phillips pleaded not guilty, stating that her husband had fallen down the stairs to his death.

The witnesses gave their direct evidence and it was compelling: the original assault brought against her by her husband; the threats on the street that it would be the rope next for her; the observations of relatives witnessing punches being thrown; and the screams and shouts heard by neighbours.

The judge's summing up was quick, as was the jury's retirement of just half an hour. The main points of the law relating to proving guilt for which the judge advised the jury, (made up of twelve men), was murder, manslaughter, or not guilty. The verdict hinged on determining the answers to some questions. Was there any intention to kill? Did the actions of the woman, in the form of her assaults, constitute a situation where the assaults may have led to death? If so, she was guilty of a manslaughter offence at least. Or was she telling the truth, namely that he fell down the stairs?

It did not take the jury long. They retired, they reappeared. The foreman stood up and said, "Guilty of wilful murder," but it was with a rider. They thought because of the woman's age she should be treated with leniency and given mercy. Mary-Ann must have made an impression in the courtroom of self-reproach and remorse as her violence and wholehearted nastiness to her husband seemed to have been diluted during the hearing.

The judge only had one option open to him. He sentenced her to death. He put on the black cap and said:

> *Mary Ann Phillips, you have been convicted of the wilful murder of your husband, after a long and patient investigation, and after a most able defence. The jury have recommended you to mercy on account of your age and sex. That recommendation will be forwarded to the Home Secretary, upon whose advice Her Majesty will determine whether it is or is not to be adopted. It is not my business to cause you needless pain by commenting on the dreadful act which you have committed. It is my business to pass upon you the sentence of the law, and the sentence of the law is, and this court doth adjudge that you, Mary Ann Phillips, be taken to the place from whence you came, and from thence to a place of execution, and that there you be hanged by the neck until you are dead...*

The judge paused as the condemned reacted to his words by repeating constantly, "I am not guilty." He continued:

> *...and that your body be afterwards buried within the precincts of the prison in which you should have been last confined and may the Lord have mercy on your soul.*

It is said she left the courtroom a very depressed woman still chanting "I am not guilty." Her solicitor went to her holding cell immediately. He told her his intention was raise a petition and a plea for mercy and have the death sentence reduced to a custodial one. His grounds were that a) she was a woman; b) she was of old age (60 years); and c) the jury had requested mercy.

It had been worked out that the earliest date for Mary-Ann's execution could be Monday, 2nd April, 1888 This, as was the usual form, allowed for three Sundays after the sentence of death by the judge.

It was the Thursday prior to the execution date. A horse cab turned up at the gates of Cardiff Gaol. The gates opened and Phillips walked slowly out between two warders. The cab took them to catch the 9.20am train to Fulham, London from Cardiff General Station. Her sentence had been commuted by the British Home Secretary to a life of penal servitude in a convict prison.

One would surmise at her age, in those times, her life would soon be over, but Mary-Ann Phillips was made from sterner stuff. Remarkably, she survived 17 years of incarceration before being released from Aylesbury Prison at the age of 77 years.

She had assisted in running the bakery in the prison and became very friendly with another inmate, Florence Maybrick. Perhaps this association was prompted by the similarities of their offences. Maybrick, an American, murdered her much older husband by poisoning him with arsenic she had soaked out of flypapers. She too was sentenced to death but was reprieved. Florence was released one year before Mary-Ann. She returned to America where she wrote a book about her trial and continued to protest her innocence.

In 1905 Mary-Ann Phillips was taken to the Salvation Army home at Moira Terrace, Adamsdown, Cardiff, a place of safety for the rest of her days. She had lived to a grand old age for the times and was said to have excellent mental faculties. She continued protesting her innocence until her death two years later.

Perhaps next time you pass the old *Horse and Groom* public house in Womanby Street, (no longer a pub – now part of a club) spare a thought for William Phillips, as it was here that he met his murderous wife all those years ago. It was a marriage made in hell!

*Taken from contemporary Victorian newspapers.
Mary-Ann Phillips in court. McDougall and Thomas, witnesses.*

CHAPTER FIVE

The forgotten stories of long-forgotten people

ADELINE AMY DAVIES, 1902

Perhaps you have never heard of Adeline Amy Davies née Young, a Cardiff woman, who hit the headlines only when she was dead. She lived in Tresillian Terrace, which is still there in part today, and leads onto Dumballs Road. Observe where the road from St Mary Street now sweeps under the Newport – Cardiff railway line towards Cardiff Bay. It was once the route of the Glamorganshire Canal. The Custom House Street Bridge took town traffic over the canal between Mill Lane and the East Canal Wharf. This bridge was to be the scene of her death.

She had married Thomas Ivor Davies, a commercial traveller, mainly in furniture. Adeline had a sister, Mary, who lived with her carpenter husband at 1, Wimborne Street, Splott. There was another sister who had been in an asylum for several years.

It all went wrong for Adeline when her husband died. The money dried up and she tried her best to take on little jobs to pay the bills. This got harder and harder and she was being pressed by creditors. The most potent creditor was the town council. Adeline owed them back monies in rates. She struggled just to live let alone pay rates, but the council demanded payment. She failed to pay and the court thought the best way of punishing her and make sure she paid in the future was to send her to prison for fourteen days. This had a terrible effect on her. According to her sister and other witnesses Adeline became unstable, with severe headaches and some thought the symptoms of heart disease.

She started to pawn her belongings in an attempt to get some money together to live and pay bills. It was during this short period that a woman stole an item from Adeline that would have gained some valuable income. She told Detective Constable Albert Davies, who arrested the woman, and she was put into custody.

This, in itself, sent Adeline into a worse mental state telling the detective that she could not live with herself for putting a woman into custody, so she refused to give evidence and the charge was withdrawn.

Adeline wrote to her sister at Wimborne Street telling her that she was unhappy, the letter was 'strange' according to Mary. The handwriting not as usual, the spelling was bad and this from an intelligent woman with a fluent grasp of English.

The time was 5.30am on a Thursday 1902 and John Coughlin was going to work. As he crossed the canal bridge, (at the end of St Mary Street, pictured right), he heard a scream. He rushed to the bridge parapet and saw a woman in the water disappearing from view. She did not reappear. He called a constable who ran around to the canal bank (near where the York Hotel now stands). He saw a pair of slippers, which seemed to indicate the spot where the woman had entered the canal.

The officer took off his jacket and his shoes and jumped in the water. He eventually found Adeline and dragged her to the bank. She was wearing just a chemise and a dressing gown. The coroner's jury reached a verdict of suicide whilst temporarily insane.

The hell of coping alone, the hell of being imprisoned, the hell of impoverishment, were all too much for Adeline Amy Davies. She just got out of bed that morning and walked to the nearby canal to end her hell. She succeeded.

WICKED WILLY WILSON, 1896

You might have thought the ragamuffins who played around the streets in the centre of Victorian Cardiff would turn out to be beggars, criminals or ne'er-do-wells. The tale of Wicked Willy Wilson may show the difference between the rich and the poor in Cardiff, or you may simply think the rich were best qualified to administer law and order.

Willy Wilson had lost his parents to cholera and lived wherever he could in the hovels and courts behind St Mary Street. He had reached the age of 15 and dreamed of some sort of employment and advancement. He heard of the training ships in Bristol that would prepare young men for a life at sea or other useful employment, usually in industry. It would be impossible for him to get there other than to walk and he probably knew that would be impossible.

Bowls Butchers Shop was situated in Llandaff Road, Canton. It was a thriving business and delivered meat to a large part of Cardiff. To do this Mr Bowls had purchased a horse and trap, which was a swift way of transporting not only people but products too.

One morning Bowls set off to deal with some business in Cardiff Town Hall in St Mary Street. He made his way along Cowbridge Road and Castle Street before turning right into High Street and pulling up his horse in front of the Town Hall. He noticed some urchins playing in the street and asked one to watch over his pony and trap. One fifteen-year-old lad volunteered to undertake the task. That lad was Willy Wilson.

Ten minutes later Bowls left the Town Hall to find the horse, the trap and the lad were gone. He made enquiries in the area but there were no witnesses to what had happened. He reported it to a constable at the nearby police station.

Willy was on his way to Bristol. He managed to get as far as Lydney Road in Blakeney in Gloucestershire when he was stopped by a constable called Jones. After questioning, the officer became suspicious and took Willy into custody. The story unfolded and Cardiff police were informed.

After a week of being in the cells, Willy's youthful exuberant appearance must have changed as he was described as lifeless, ragged and dispirited. The local media called him wicked, a 'scapegrace', and as a modern day Dick Turpin.

The magistrates in Cardiff heard the lad in tears say guilty. They refused to send him to a training ship or similar establishment as he looked physically unsuited for it. Their sentence was 14 days hard labour in prison. On release Willy would probably have been sent to the workhouse.

The magistrates went home for their lunch, and the 15-year-old, parentless, homeless, Willy went to the cells to await transporting to prison. Research reveals no more on Wicked Willy Wilson.

THE MAN WHO WOULD BE KING, 1861

Stand by *The Queens Hotel* in St Mary Street and think back one and a half centuries. Behind the façade were several courts mostly inhabited by impoverished people, in fact as early as 1900 these were being called hovels.

Born into squalor in 1861 in Landore Court was a baby to the Sexton family, Daniel. The name Sexton means 'Church Warden' but its origins are French and Latin too. In researching the family, it appears that the Sextons came from Ireland, probably County Limerick, during the Great Famine that ran from 1845-51. Their poor background appeared to be no barrier to a family that raised a fine young man who was out and about looking for work in his early teens. Young Daniel Sexton must have looked the part, dressed well and of some advanced intellect as he found his niche in the French Consulate, which at that time was situated in Bute Street, Cardiff. It would appear he learnt a little French before applying for the job and while he worked there as a clerk managed to master French fluently.

Sexton was restless and he wanted advancement. He learnt other European languages, it appeared they came naturally to him. At the age of 19 years he applied to be an officer in the Metropolitan Police in London, something that may have scared other men of his age. Cardiff was a big and bustling town but London was on a different scale both in population, job prospects, and, of course, crime.

He was successful and within a year he made the rank of detective. He became the chosen one when it came to investigations that involved languages, especially in the early days when he was often to be found in Paris on enquiries. The Chief of Detectives in the Met during the mid-1880s sent Sexton all over France undertaking enquiries and observations of suspects.

In those days, it was Soho that was the most popular inner city area for French-speaking people in London to congregate and live, and that meant that Sexton spent many months of his duties in that area. It was not only French that Sexton was noted for. He was also sent to work in Hatton Gardens amongst the German colony, and in Saffron Hill amongst the Italians. He spoke both of these languages fluently.

At the age of just 30 years he was promoted to Detective Inspector in 1891, and became one of the youngest men ever to attain that rank. His exploits in crime fighting made him famous – not only in Scotland Yard but in his home town of Cardiff.

He had arrested a Frenchman, Guerin, in London on an Extradition Warrant from a French police force. Guerin was sent to the infamous Devil's Island prison camp in French Guiana. Its real name was *Bagne de Cayenne* (Cayenne Prison) and it became famous in later years in the movie *Papillon*. Its reputation was enough to send shivers down the spine of any convict and general opinion considers it to be the worst penal establishment ever.

Guerin escaped and subsequently ended up in Jersey. He was later recognised and arrested and held in custody. It was Detective Inspector Sexton's job to go to there and transport him to London in readiness for his return to Devil's Island. With the Extradition Order safely in his possession Sexton went on the long trip to Jersey and arrested his man. They knew each other well.

The Frenchman said, on seeing Sexton, "You won't get me back to Devil's Island."

Sexton smiled and replied, "We shall see."

Things went well until the both men were in a compartment of a train taking them to London. The powerfully-built Frenchman suddenly opened the carriage door of the train travelling at 60mph and tried to jump out. Sexton jumped up and stopped him from leaping out of the train. A fight followed that saw both Guerin and Sexton coming to blows and struggling in the open doorway. The carriage door was swinging back and forth into the men. Guerin managed to climb out on to the running board of the train, outside of the carriage. Sexton, still holding onto the swinging door, continued the struggle and tried to prevent his prisoner being killed from falling off the fast-moving train.

After several minutes, Guerin was dragged into the carriage and subdued. He threatened to murder the officer should he get the chance, and jump out again if he could. One can imagine that Sexton drew upon the train staff for assistance at that point as it is known that Guerin did appear at Bow Street and was extradited.

There were numerous other incidents bringing the name of Sexton to the notice of the chiefs of police both in London and various other capitals in Europe. Even simple arrests seemed to turned nasty on many occasions.

Arresting a foreigner in Bloomsbury, London, for a European police force Sexton had to fight off a bulldog as well, which was biting and clinging to him. Not once did he let go of his prisoner, who was subsequently conveyed to a police station.

He was decorated by the French Government for his services in the extradition of offenders. He had numerous commendations from Chiefs of Police and Ministers in various European countries and many times from the Commissioner of the Metropolitan Police.

In 1902, at the age of 42, he appeared before the Royal Commission of Alien Immigration and his contributions were invaluable to law-making at the time.

Sexton retired from the police at the age of 49 on a full and well-justified pension, but retirement did not last long. He died soon after his police career ended with the cause of death being an internal injury sustained in a fight some years earlier.

NEIGHBOURHOOD WATCH, CANTON-STYLE, 1855.

In the nineteenth century Canton was growing. Houses were being constructed at a fast rate and even as early as 1855 it was described as a 'thickly-populated suburb' by local newspapers. With the newly-built housing came the usual problem that owners have encountered for millennia – burglaries! It was becoming a major problem for residents as there did not seem anything the small band of borough constables was doing about it.

The lot of residents was not a happy one because as with the growth of housing came the growth of alehouses, shebeens, and disorderly houses. Canton was reflecting the conditions of the Central area where drunkenness was a major social problem. The few detectives around in those days would have been fully tied up with enquiries and would have appeared to be entirely reactive rather than pro-active. Who could possibly protect the residents from gangs of burglars at work during the hours of darkness in Canton?

In an early form of a Neighbourhood Watch the residents decided to fight the problem for themselves. Many got together and decided to work shifts as community detectives. As a local journalist mentioned at the time, "…several of the most bold and courageous residents have, during the last week or two, volunteered for the safety of Canton to maintain watch and ward, during the dreary hours of night."

Nearly all the burglaries were occurring during the night, so it was through the hours of darkness that they decided to put together shifts of volunteers. It was a hard job when combined with awful weather, the lack of any street lighting, or the threat of violence, it must have been unpleasant when, after a knock on the door, a fellow volunteer said, "Your turn on nights". Night after night they failed to catch a single burglar as the shadowy streets aided the criminals.

In the early hours of one morning two of the brave residents heard sounds coming from a warehouse-type construction at the end of Wyndham Street. They crept up, hiding the flare from their lanterns, and peeped through the window. Bringing their lanterns up and holding them to get light inside the building they shouted "Surrender or die!"

They were faced with the rather unusual sight of a borough police constable 'enjoying himself' with a local girl! On seeing the lights, he jumped up, and ran, (one would imagine pulling up his trousers as he did so), to get out of the building. He then fell into a building ditch. The chasers did not want to jump into the ditch in the night, but the constable managed to scramble out and made good his escape. The young lady was not named in any report, perhaps for the best, as she would have been in a lot of trouble in mid Victorian Britain.

THE ATTEMPTED MURDER OF THE REVEREND FATHER MICHAEL GAVIN GARELLI

The Roman Catholic Church had a bumpy ride during the first century of modern Cardiff, between 1801 and 1901. With the influx of Irish immigrants, during the first half of the century, the Anglican and Non-Conformists were opposed to the Roman Catholic church. It did not manifest itself in public disorder, but there were people diametrically opposed to the furtherance of Catholicism.

Several constables were called to Andrews Hall one evening in 1881, when a former Catholic priest started his anti-Catholic diatribe. There were scuffles and the police had to eject a number of men from the packed venue.

Over the years the two religions gradually adopted a more harmonious association. Several Catholic presbyteries and churches were constructed in the Irish residential areas for worship and pastoral care. However, Cardiff was a dangerous place and even a priest had to be careful on the street.

The year is 1871. John James Sullivan resided in Mary Ann

Street, central Cardiff, at a time when it had the reputation of being the most crime ridden and violent road in Cardiff. The area was riddled with licensed pubs and shebeens (un-licenced drinking dens), but nearby was a beacon of light, the Roman Catholic Church in David Street. In between periods of working at sea, Sullivan worshipped at the church and also St Peter's Roman Catholic church in Roath.

The Reverend Father Michael Garrelli had officiated at ceremonies at both churches. He had recently arrived in Cardiff from Holland. It appears he did not get on with Sullivan. Sullivan had a police record and was certainly an unstable character. He told associates that the priest was going to strike him dumb and blind. It had been noted by other worshippers at St Peter's that Sullivan was mentally unstable and had to be watched. He had been overheard to threaten "…to do for some of the clergy."

These were extremely difficult times – crime and drunkenness were rampant and no doubt the Catholic priests had their hands full undertaking their daily duties. Poverty seemed to be at the root of most of the troubles and the church had an important part to play in pastoral care. Amongst their congregations, there lurked trouble and John James Sullivan was soon to be at the vanguard of it.

In July 1871, Sullivan took work on a merchant ship on the short journey to France and back. He returned to worship at Father Garelli's church. There is no doubt that Sullivan was disrupting services with constant chatter and had to be disciplined by the priests. On several occasions, he said his prayers out loud to the annoyance of other worshippers and when told not to do so he threatened all and sundry within the church of being shot! One priest did not admit him into the church because of his behaviour, which later Sullivan explained away by saying he was reacting to the threats of the clergy of being sent to the curse of God in Hell.

A few days later Fathers Garelli and Cornoedus had occasion to visit parishioners near the Pier Head at the southern end of Bute Street. The Rev James Cornoedus was a professor of French at

Ratcliffe R.C. College in Leicester. University. At noon, they made their way back up Bute Street towards their church. They walked as far as the Bute West Dock canal feeder bridge, then known as North and Lowes Bridge, where they saw Sullivan walking towards them. There then followed a strange turn of events.

*The North & Lowes Bridge taken in the 1970s.
The site of the shooting a century earlier.*

Sullivan, muttering something, had just passed them, when some children nearby saw him take a pistol from his coat and aim it at Father Garelli. The children shouted a warning. Sullivan pulled the trigger, but the gun failed to fire. Garelli turned and saw the weapon in Sullivan's hand and that it was pointing at him. Garelli, in an act of either bravery or stupidity, walked towards the man and tried to take the gun from him. He failed to do so. After his failure Garelli turned his back on Sullivan and carried on with his journey! Not a wise thing to do.

The children shouted again, and the priest wheeled around and saw Sullivan pointing the weapon directly at him once again. Sullivan fired and Garelli felt a pain in his arm. Sullivan then threw the pistol into the canal. Father Garelli noticed that his own clothes were damaged and there was blood oozing from a graze on his arm. He had been lucky, although Sullivan had aimed at his body, the shouts of the children and his quick movement had prevented a more serious injury… or even death.

There then followed a surreal journey to the police station, Sullivan doing as he was told, walking meekly alongside the injured priest.

There was another witness to the incident, John Davies, the landlord of *The Admiral Napier* public house. He had seen the whole incident. He had also seen Sullivan load the gun the second time. He watched the bullet bounce off the wall and roll into the gutter. It appeared it was a percussion cap pistol, which required single loading, an outdated method even then.

There was a canal lock nearby and Charles Barclay, the keeper, managed to recover the weapon from the canal. This could not have been an easy job.

As is usual, an arrested individual sees things differently. He told the police that Father Garelli had insulted and threatened him. Garelli had warned him that he would soon be struck blind and dumb. When he saw the priest walking towards him in Bute Street he decided to see if the Reverend Father could carry out that threat. He took out the gun, which he thought was not loaded, there was a struggle, and the gun went off. He said he had not meant any offence, just to see if there was the Holy power to strike him blind when the priest was subjected to a threat. Father Cornoedus verified all that his associate had stated, and added that he had seen the first shot misfire and witnessed the second shot hit the arm of Father Garelli.

Sullivan was committed to the Assize Court. A Grand Jury was sworn in. This system of choosing a Grand Jury of local citizens was abolished in 1933 in Great Britain as it was seen as no more than a method for assisting the prosecution by cherry-picking establishment figures or people of certain political persuasions. In fact, the Grand Jury at this Assize was made up entirely of men, as was the norm. Running through their names it is obvious they were all people of substance from the affluent areas.

At court a month later a Doctor told the jury that Sullivan thought he had died and gone to heaven and God was his father and mother. He also stated he had hanged himself in Cork but came back to life again. Even though he was obviously insane, the charges were still put to him. The jury found him guilty of grievous bodily harm but recommended mercy. He was remanded but later at another court received twelve months' imprisonment. *The Cardiff Times* reported:

> *The extraordinary case of the Assizes, which we have already alluded to, is the shooting at a Roman Catholic Priest, by a Roman Catholic Irishman, in the public streets. Sometimes Irishmen at home forget themselves and take aim at a landlord or a peeler, "just to enforce the fiat of a home rule" movement. But to fire at a priest from Old Ireland is free from that species of sacrilege as yet. Remembering the proverbial respect and veneration in which Roman Catholic clergymen are held by the Irish people, we should deem it strange if Mr John Sullivan were really responsible for his conduct on the 18th of August, when he fired in the Bute Road at the Rev Mr Garelli. Before the twelve months' imprisonment expires, it will probably be ascertained beyond doubt that the Rev gentleman's assailant is deranged.*

The work of a priest in the most troubled times of Cardiff's growth must have been laborious to say the least. The Reverend Father Garelli's work amongst the poverty-ridden families was stressful and now he had to come to terms with a deranged worshipper attempting to assassinate him. No doubt the priest would have carried on working hard at his particular front line, but he must have been very wary in the future when disciplining noisy worshippers.

* * *

Crwys Road Police Station, Cathays, 2017. Cell block now unused. If cell gates could talk!

CHAPTER SIX

The Llanrumney Hall murder

The Hall as it would have looked at the time of the murder.

> Warning:
> The last few pages of this chapter graphically document an execution and may make harrowing reading.

The finding of guilt by magistrates or a jury is always based on the evidence presented to them by a police investigation. If the trial is of an individual charged with murder then the evidence must be watertight and leave no chance for mistake or unfair conviction. If the death penalty was the only sentence that a judge could deliver then it was imperative that the conviction was safe beyond all reasonable doubt. But, is such certainty possible?

There are instances in the United Kingdom where an innocent man or woman has gone to the gallows. One can only imagine the feelings of injustice when one of these sad individuals was led to their legally-constituted death.

It appears that the media, the prison authorities, and the executioners were keen to tell the public when a hanging went according to plan. It seemed that the public felt reassured by the words: "The execution was quickly carried out, and without a scene or hitch of any kind." This reassurance was nothing to do with the establishment, the prison personnel, or indeed the judiciary, but it was all to do with the calmness and state of mind of the convicted felon.

Some accepted their fate, as well as acknowledging their conviction for murder, and took the punishment as a consequence of their own making. Time and time again one reads that the convict accepted the sentence and walked with head held high to the gallows. Without the media being present to witness the hanging this may not have always been the case.

There were times when any compassionate reader of the local newspapers may be been brought to tears as a reporter tells of the last few minutes of a condemned man or woman's life.

It certainly was in the case of James Henry Gibbs, who

protested his innocence of murder from the first minute of his arrest until the last minute of his life. The evidence seemed to be quite conclusive yet was wholly circumstantial.

This rather evocative and emotional letter by Gibbs was sent at the end of his murder trial. Gibbs stated in court in no uncertain terms that he was innocent of the murder of his wife. It did not help Gibbs' state of mind having family problems that are reflected in his last written words.

Usk Gaol, 23rd August, 1874.
My dear Father and Mother, Sister and Brother, Relations and Friends all. I send these few lines in answer to your kind and affectionate letter, which I received this morning. I was very glad to hear from you. I have been expecting to hear from you this last few days, in answer to a letter which I had written to you, and it was not until this morning that I was told that the letter has not been sent, which disappointed me greatly, and so that you will not know what I wished you to. But never mind, my dear parents; I trust in God for His mercy and pardon. I know, my dear parents, this has been a great trial to us all; but there is still a greater one awaits us, and where no witness is required. It is of no use now of my asking you anything that I had a wish to, because I shall never in this world hear or see anything of you again but I do earnestly pray to God for us one and all to meet again in heaven, and where true joy and happiness is only to be found. As regards my health, I am as well as ever I was. I trust to God that He will make the light of His face to shine upon you all, and give you health and strength to you all, that you may never know what trouble is. After this, I ask my dear brother and sister to be kind and affectionate to each other, particularly to theirs and my dear parents. Trust in God and He will be with you. It is a very hard thing for me to know the hour of my

death; but, my dear parents, it is a very happy thing for me to know that I die quite an innocent man for what I am accused of. I have met with great kindness throughout this trial, which has been a great help to me. Now, with my fondest and affectionate love to you all, and wishing you good-bye for ever in this world, I remain your unfortunate son and brother, nephew and cousin, friend and acquaintance, but thank God very innocent of what I am accused of.
JAMES HENRY GIBBS.
Farewell. Farewell. Farewell.
Good-bye; God bless you all."

Llanrumney today is a sprawling suburb of Cardiff, much bigger in population than many towns across Wales. It was originally rural farmland with cottages dotted about, inhabited by farm labourers and their families. The most impressive building, still standing today is Llanrumney Hall, built in Elizabethan times (some put the date as 1460 A.D.). It has had many distinguished owners over the centuries, none more famous than Captain Henry Morgan.

It was in 1859 that Mr Charles Williams of Roath Court bought the estate. Then you would have approached the house down a very long drive from what is now the A48. There were orchards, flower gardens, and a superb walled garden within the extensive 700 acres of parkland that surrounded the mansion. Llanrumney Farm was situated to the west of the mansion.

Near the Rumney River was also a corn mill and a millpond. Many of the field boundaries were lined by ancient oak trees and in summer the fields and hedgerows were populated by numerous species of wild flowers.

Wednesday 3rd June, 1874 was a beautiful day, bright and sunny from the start, but what farmer John Hughes was about to find would bring his day crashing around him. He took for granted during his rounds, checking fences and flock, that the smells of the countryside would be as they always were, a mixture of aromatic flowers and the distinctive smell of the animals in the fields. On this morning, however, something was wrong. There was a strange smell in the air. It did not just disturb Hughes but also his dog, who was showing signs of uneasiness. The behaviour of the dog was of concern in the mind of the farmer when it refused to obey commands and became increasingly agitated.

The dog was barking at an overgrown section of hedgerow between two fields. The farmer expected there to be some animal of some sort in hiding, perhaps a fox. He encouraged the dog to go into the hedge, but the dog would not obey his order.

The only way for the man to check out the problem was to walk around to the other side of it. He followed a well-worn path along to a gate then returned on the other side. He pushed his way into the hedge, forcing apart the thick undergrowth and ivy. Then, he saw the decomposing body of a woman. It was a truly horrific sight that caused the man to recoil in disgust.

As any inquiring detective will tell you, one of the worst sites to be seen on a tour of duty is a human body that is undergoing the decomposition process. This is amplified if the deceased has been left on open ground and is subject to interference by the weather, and animal and insect life.

The farmer ran, as if for his life, to report his grisly find. The police were summoned and in turn they called for a medical man to examine the body at the scene. Dr Loughor from Roath attended.

He noted that the body was that of a woman in an advanced state of decomposition and lying on her back with one arm across her chest. He noted that the neck had been eaten away as were most of the other internal organs. He also noted blood staining on some stones in the hedgerow near the body. Grasped tightly in one hand was a piece of fern leading the doctor to surmise that just prior to death she was clutching at anything. The deceased was taller than average and dressed in white and red petticoats, a faded brown dress, a black velveteen jacket, and a red flannel coat.

The body was taken away for a post mortem, which was

undertaken by Lougher and attended by PC Hughes. It revealed that many of the internal organs were missing having been preyed on by insects. The petticoats of the deceased were drenched with blood and the doctor ascertained that because of the position of the body the blood had originated from the neck area, therefore giving his belief that her throat was cut. He found a bruise on one hand and some bruising to the leg. This he surmised though may have been caused by the steel in her petticoats. He estimated that the woman had probably been dead around three weeks. The fern in her hand showed that she was still alive when dragged to the hedge, there was no other explanation, as there were also traces of fern on her clothing.

One can imagine the furious police activity that took place after the finding of the body. Llanrumney was a rural area and the local police station was situated at St Mellons, covered by the Monmouthshire Constabulary.

The identification of the body was made by staff who had seen the woman calling at the Hall weeks before. The name of the deceased was Susan Ingram. The events leading up to her murder are described later.

Sergeant Hale was brought down from Risca to help in the investigation and it was he, along with Inspector Sheppard, who attended at the work place of one James Henry Gibbs. He was a butler at Llanrumney Hall and suspicion towards him had been aroused. After extended conversations with Williams, (the owner of the Hall), the police searched the butler's quarters. Hale used a step-ladder to check on the top of cupboard in the pantry and found an umbrella and a parcel of clothing. The following days' search of the same area resulted in Hale finding razors and blades. There was no evidence of blood on any of the razors or blades.

The police enquiry commenced into possible murder suspects. Forensics were very basic compared to today but there were still investigatory techniques that centred on science. Nearly all the detective work was done by what many would call 'good old fashioned coppering', that is knocking doors, asking questions, following hunches, and local knowledge.

There were four staff at Llanrumney Hall in the 1870s; a cook/housekeeper, a coachman, housemaid, and butler/footman. Many of their duties doubled into others. It must have been quite an easy existence for the staff. The owner, Mr Williams, was often away, therefore the staff undertook their employ at their own pace and with no deadlines. After the coachman had taken his employer off to the railway station they all knew the return date when they would see their master again. It must have been like a holiday to be able to pace oneself in furtherance of their duties. One man seemed to be mentioned more than others as an "unknown quantity" and that man was James Henry Gibbs, the butler-cum-footman.

Enquiries revealed a Susan Ann Ingram, once a servant at the Hall, had been replaced by another young girl, this time living locally in St Mellons, called Mary Jones. Gibbs had met Mary Jones at a concert at the National School in St Mellons. He had instantly been attracted to her and, it seems, her to him. In the weeks that followed he was often seen at her home, to such an extent that her parents soon regarded Gibbs as likely to be their daughter's future husband. He was a charming man.

The owner of the Hall was often in Scotland on long shooting expeditions, therefore Gibbs used his freedom to visit Mary, spending many hours there several times a week.

Detectives found out that the staff at Llanrumney Hall knew nothing about the activities of their colleague. He seemed to lie at the drop of a hat, which did not help in finding out what they really wanted to know: his past history; where he had come from; and a few insights into his previous life. Detectives did not trust him one bit. The only items of interest they managed to glean about his history were one or two of his previous places of employment. They found that when he claimed he was a butler he had in fact been a footman, this with several previous employers.

The complicated life of Gibbs was compounded by deceit and dishonesty and is best understood and explained by a journalist who, at the time, followed every twist and turn of the subsequent murder trial from the discovery of the body until the condemned man's last day.

It is to be noted that after leaving Llanrumney Hall, Susan Ingram, the erstwhile servant, took up employment in Weybridge, Surrey, as a servant to a Mrs Heathfield. These are the journalist's words:

> *Gibbs had a great deal of leisure time, which he spent partly at the house of Miss Jones and partly in concocting a scheme for marrying his former fellow servant, Susan Ingram. While visiting Miss Jones, he was constantly writing to Miss Ingram, and he began a kind of double life, into which his duplicity of character had led him. Whatever motive can be given as an excuse for adopting this course it must have been a bad one. Miss Ingram had a little money in the Post-office Savings Bank, and he knew it. She was desirous of leaving service and commencing in some business. So was he. The whole arrangements for the marriage were carried on by letter, for he never went to see her at Weybridge until he took her to Jersey. Mrs Heathfield entertained a very high opinion of and great respect for Miss Ingram, and when Susan stated her intention of getting married (in Jersey) she made some inquiries, and endeavoured to persuade her cook to give up all thoughts of it. (She did not trust Gibbs). Finding this useless, she next desired that the marriage should take place at Weybridge, but to this Gibbs strongly objected. Miss Ingram wished to be married in England. Gibbs refused, and she gave way, but not until she had exhausted all her powers of persuasion. She had a great dread of the voyage, as the vessel in which she came to England with Mrs Noiton was nearly lost crossing the Channel. She also objected on the ground of expense. It was of no use, he had resolved that they should get married in Jersey, and she drew out £30*

> *to pay his fare to London and their expenses to and from Jersey. Mrs Heathfield had left home before Susan Ingram left her service, when Gibbs on the 24th of July, 1873, called for her, and they at once proceeded to Southampton and thence to Jersey.*

It was in Jersey they married, and Susan Ingram became Susan Gibbs. On arriving in Jersey, Miss Ingram went to the residence of Mrs Norman, her sister, at St Hillier's, and Gibbs stayed at *The Imperial Hotel*, St Saviour's. It was from this place, after making arrangements for the marriage to Miss Ingram, that he wrote the letter to Miss Mary Ann Jones, and expressed a hope to be back on the following week.

On the 30th of July Gibbs and Ingram were married at St Saviour's Church, and on the 5th of August, after a residence of twelve days on the island, he left for Wales. He desired that she should remain with her sister, Mrs Norman, while he returned to Wales alone, alleging as his reason that Mr Williams would dismiss him from service if he knew that he was a married man. She was not happy with that and they travelled to Southampton the same day, proceeded to London, stayed there that night, and then left for the Cardiff the next morning.

They arrived in Cardiff on the evening of 6th August. Gibbs took his wife to *Elliott's Hotel,* on St Mary Street, and he left at once for Llanrumney Hall. Later that night he went to the house of Mary Jones and remained there some hours.

Mrs Gibbs stayed at Elliott's Hotel for three days, and Gibbs did not go once to see her. Alone, and a stranger to the place, she described her life as miserable. Portions of each night were spent in tears. She could not sleep because the noise and bustle of the town kept her awake, and on one night a drunken brawl outside the house much increased her terror, and she was determined to leave as soon as possible and seek a quiet, private lodging.

She knew her husband could not take her to Llanrumney Hall so she resolved upon entering service as a cook at some place in, or near, her lodging, and for this purpose she applied at Mrs Pedler's Registry Office (an employment agency for finding staff), on John Street. She hoped for a situation as cook in a gentleman's family. Here she met a daughter of Sergeant Wallbridge, and on explaining her desire to find some private lodgings. she was taken to Mrs Mahoney, of Dispensary Court, who was well known to Sergeant Wallbridge and was at once taken in as a lodger. Now her next task was to find work.

She told her husband all about it and Gibbs impressed on her the necessity for keeping their marriage a secret, urging that he would lose his place if she did not. At his request, she called herself Mrs Ingram. It was by this name she was known at *Elliott's Hotel* and was the same name she gave at the Registry Office and to Mrs Mahoney.

Days passed in her new lodgings at Dispensary Court and there seemed to be little chance of her finding a job. Her money was diminishing so she availed herself of a suggestion of Mrs Mahoney. She went out cooking at some of the public establishments of the town, and as this was not frequent work, she also took on some cleaning jobs.

These were hard days of toil for her. She had never been accustomed to hard work, and the skin of her hands peeled off in places, either from the action of strong soda and water, or from the bristles of the brushes. She frequently came home tired and with aching limbs. She was sometimes unable to resume her work on the following day and this brought with it the reputation of unreliability.

Mrs Mahoney, her landlady, was a widow over 70 years of age, said to be poor, honest, and extremely kind. She acted the part of a mother to Mrs Gibbs, when she was feeling depressed at not seeing her husband. The only form of communication between husband and wife was by letter and she knew she could not post one to the Hall. Mrs Mahoney did her best but was angry at James Gibbs' neglect of his wife.

At first James had called to see Susan frequently, perhaps once or twice a week and on each occasion he took money from her. Her hard, domestic work brought in some money, which she saved, she hardly spent any of it, except on rent and subsistence.

The smiling, affable and apparently reliable Llanrumney Hall butler took on a double life. On one occasion, he went to Mrs Mahoney's house and found his wife was very unwell. He told her that he had to meet his master in an hour. He left a pair of boots to be repaired and asked her to go and fetch them for him, and pay for them as he had no money. She did so, but had to borrow money for the purpose, and the next day went to work to earn its replacement, although she had intended to rest.

It appears Susan Gibbs was a quiet woman. She frequently attended St John's Church. One thing was for sure, Mrs Gibbs was very fond of her husband, and did not see any faults in him.

On another occasion, he said that he wanted to go and visit his father for a few days but had no money. She went to the bank and drew cash out. It appears from Mrs Mahoney's testimony that she was happy to see him happy and willingly gave him the money. Susan found out that he was going on Tuesday morning and went down to the railway station to see him off. She had found out the train times and waited there to surprise him. He certainly got a surprise when she approached him… after seeing him buy two tickets!

She questioned him and he walked towards Mary Jones, the current servant at the Hall, and his lover. He told Susan that Mary, also an employee working at Llanrumney Hall, was afraid of travelling anywhere on her own and she was also going on the train, so he had offered to assist her. Susan watched her husband and Mary get into a carriage compartment. He lowered the window and kissed his wife goodbye as the train pulled away.

There is a debate as to what happened at the station. On police questioning there was a suggestion that there was a 'domestic scene' on the station and an argument, with claim and counter-claim. This was found to be not true at a later court hearing. At that later point, Susan was dead and could not give her own story.

The police, through the examination of Mrs Mahoney, (Susan's landlady), seemingly verified it was unlikely there was a scene at the station as claimed by station staff. Mahoney told detectives that when Susan arrived back at the lodgings she praised her husband for his gentlemanly conduct in purchasing a ticket and assisting a vulnerable young woman.

The landlady's reaction was one perhaps the police had themselves: she laughed! She told her gullible lodger that he seemed kinder to everyone else than he was toward her. She even questioned why James Gibbs had not asked his own wife to go with him.

Susan was angry. She did not like anyone running down her husband and hated the innuendos. Mrs Mahoney said she would speak to James on his return, but Susan pleaded with her not to, saying he was highly-strung and vulnerable and may harm himself with such accusations.

The police later found other witnesses to interview and extremely convincing witnesses too. Mrs Mahoney had neighbours at her lodging house at Dispensary Court, a Mrs Wilson and her children, and they became the best of friends with Susan Gibbs. Wilson's husband was a police officer and one of his friends was Constable Hughes at St Mellons Police Station. The tangled web began to unfold and as every police officer knows, when chatting with fellow officers, all sorts of local intelligence is discussed.

Wilson was informed that Miles, the coachman at the Hall, believed that Gibbs was married and had on one occasion told him his suspicion. It was denied. Miles had no time for Gibbs and did not trust him. He had seen Gibbs going to Mary Jones' house on numerous occasions. Hughes told Wilson that everyone at the Hall believed Gibbs was married and they had even obtained descriptions of his suspected wife. These descriptions matched Constable Wilson's next door neighbour, Susan Gibbs. Miles decided to write a letter to Susan at Dispensary Court.

Susan Gibbs went to the Hall. On her way through the lanes

she asked Martin, the gardener, for directions but really it was to ask him if he knew whether James Gibbs was working that day. Staff at the Hall saw the conversation with the gardener taking place from an upstairs window. One can imagine the excitement of the cook and the housemaid when they saw Susan Gibbs approaching. They ran downstairs and waited in an adjacent room for the bell to ring. They said in later interviews that they had intended to take Susan to the kitchen and then bring in her husband, James. They wanted it sorted out and probably were loving the excitement of the whole situation.

But there was a problem. James Gibbs saw her coming too and got to the door before the bell rang. He told his wife to ask for a Mr Smith, leave immediately, and then go back to her lodgings.

The devious man then went into the room and spoke to the two women. He told them a woman had called asking for a Mr Smith. They both shouted at him, accusing the woman of being his wife. James Gibbs said "May God strike me dead if I am married."

He left the Hall and ran after Susan explaining his actions as on account of being scared of losing his job if his employer knew he was married. Once they had passed the farmhouse and left the driveway of Llanrumney Hall he walked with her some of the way back to the centre of Cardiff.

The police knew of these events at the Hall and her walk home from several witnesses. Three prime witnesses, the cook and the housekeeper, another Martin the gardener. The main one was Mrs Wilson, the constable's wife, living in Dispensary Court, in the centre of Cardiff. Susan Gibbs had returned home and told her all about it.

The letter from the coachman, Miles, had done the trick. Susan replied saying that she would be calling at the Hall. Both Constable Wilson and his wife had discussed the situation of their neighbour and both were convinced all was not right. They were too afraid to mention it to her as she already seemed very unhappy and they did not want to make it worse by adding their suspicions.

Things were going from bad to worse for James Henry Gibbs.

Mary Jones' parents had found out that the man their daughter was seeing was probably married. The police were told that one evening the three of them, mother, father, and Mary told Gibbs in no uncertain terms of their suspicions. They said in their statements that Gibbs dropped to his knees and swore he was not. He went further. He said that the woman calling at the Hall was a loose woman who had her eyes on Miles the coachman.

Gibbs made his way to see his wife and, apparently, she showed him the letter from Miles. He said simply "It's a forgery." He then went on to say, in the hearing of Mrs Mahoney that, "St Mellons is an area full of liars, ne'r-do-wells and awful people."

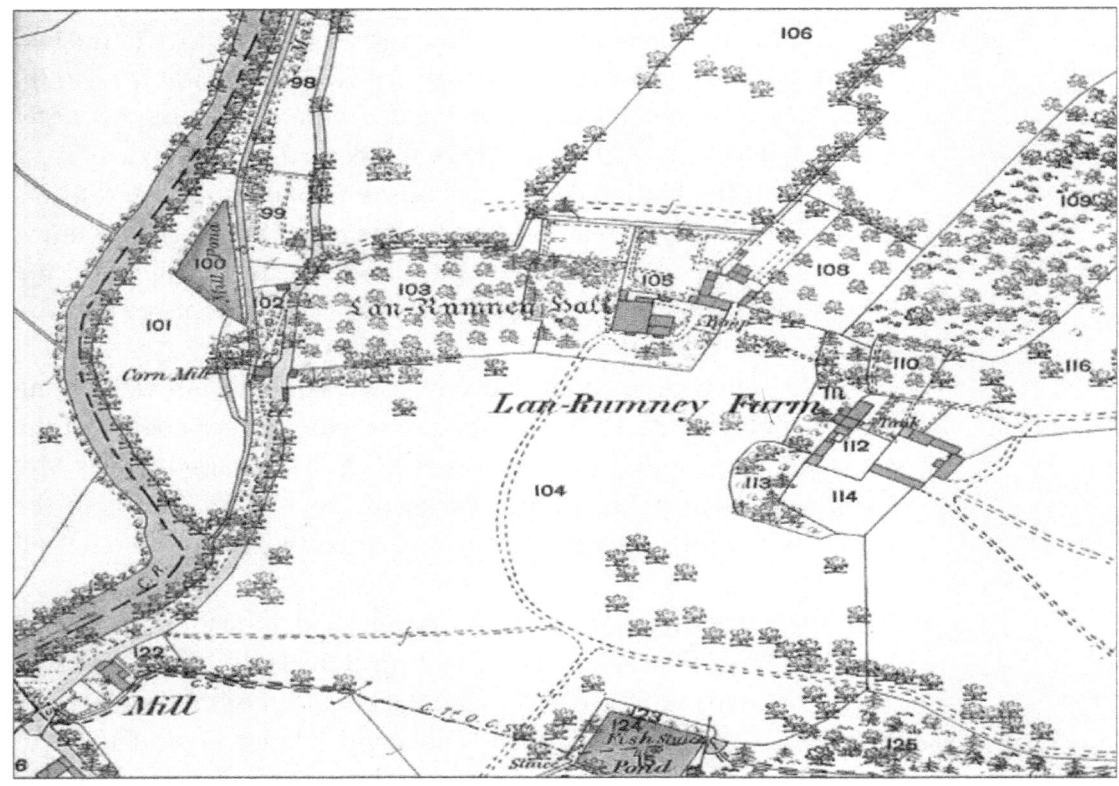

The Hall is at the centre. Fish ponds to the south. Showing farms and the River Rumney.

Susan Gibbs was in a state. She wanted to believe her husband's explanations and wish the whole thing away. She knew he was a God fearing man and a committed Christian and would rather believe him than all the other nasty people who had been plying her with their painful suspicions. Police were told that Susan decided to believe her husband not the "…nasty people of St Mellons." St Mellons residents had been all tarred with a rather nasty brush by Gibbs and it is surely naïvety in the extreme to believe him, but that is exactly what Susan did.

Particulars are a little sketchy but it then appears via police enquiry and the memory of Miles that one night, on either the 12th or 13th May, Gibbs arrived back at the Hall very late, circa 1.30am. It was Miles who let him in, and Gibbs hardly spoke. Miles noted that he went out again within a few minutes. This was a very important piece of evidence against Gibbs for the subsequent charges against him. It is known that he returned not long after this time with his umbrella, which he hid on top of the pantry cupboard.

There then followed letters written by Gibbs to his wife's close friends telling one of them that she had gone to live in Reading, and to another that she had taken up residence in St Mellons. There was no-one who could verify the assertions and enquiries revealed in St Mellons that there was no-one who knew of such a woman in residence.

Behind the scenes, it appeared that Gibbs was planning his marriage to Miss Jones even after denying venomously he was married.

It was the grisly find by the farmer of Susan Gibbs' decomposing body in the ditch near the Hall kick-started the official police enquiry.

When Gibbs was arrested on suspicion of murdering the woman found in the ditch, his clothes were sent to an expert in Newport who ascertained that his jacket had been thoroughly washed – but not well enough. Blood stains were found in various parts. Whether the stains were animal or human in origin would have been impossible to determine without chemical analysis techniques that did not yet exist. Blood stains were also discovered on Gibbs' trousers, but, of course the analyst could not confirm that the blood was human. Today blood samples can be proven as coming from a specific individual, not so then, so even though of the greatest evidential interest, Gibbs could easily present his own version of events relating to the stains.

A good insight into the character and personality of the murdered woman comes from another report at the time. After the discovery of the murder, Mrs Heathfield (Susan's previous employer from Weybridge) had written letters to Mrs Mahoney (Susan's ex-landlady in Cardiff) stating her shock at the events and praising her ex-employee. One of the letters reads:

> *I was always afraid that the marriage would not turn out for the happiness of poor Susan. She was a most faithful and affectionate creature, and I entertained a very sincere regard for her, and for her many amiable and good qualities. That her husband could be so wicked, I never suspected. Ingram was a true Christian, and was thus somewhat prepared for her sudden fate."*

In another letter, she says:

> *I never saw him, as he came to fetch her away when I was absent. Ingram lived in the service of a gentleman at Lymington, Hampshire, and it was from that place that I received her character. I valued her much for her faithful services, and as she was a true Christian I feel a comfort in the hope that she was not at the time unprepared to enter upon eternity."*

There was an inquest of Susan Gibbs (née Ingram) on 6th June, 1874 and the Coroner's Court committed James Henry Gibbs to the local Assize Court for trial on a charge of the murder of his wife. Monmouth Town Hall was the location of the Assizes where trials were undertaken under the auspices of a High Court Judge.

It was on the 6th August, 1874 that Gibbs stood trial in front of Judge Mr Justice Lush and a local Monmouthshire jury. The sensational story surrounding the murder guaranteed that the square outside the building was packed with people, all hoping to get into the public gallery, but that was always full.

The trial started with a short summary. Gibbs was the husband of the dead woman and was in full time employment at Llanrumney Hall as Mr Williams' butler. Not far from Llanrumney Hall was the little village of St Mellons with its 100 or so residents. It was one of these residents that Gibbs was interested in, a young lady by the name of Mary Jones. Mrs Gibbs found out about the burgeoning liaison between her husband and Miss Jones and many an argument had taken place. She even attended at the Hall where she found out that her husband was in the employ of Mr Williams as a single man. It was said that Gibbs and his wife were quarrelling one day early in May in a public lane near St Mellons. The arguments got out of control and it is said that he attacked his wife and killed her. He then dragged her body into a field and secreted it.

An astounding fact was turned up by the police once the body had been found and identified. Gibbs had given notice at the Registrar's Office in Cardiff of his intended marriage to Miss Jones. This notice was posted just a few days after it was alleged he murdered his wife!

The trial that followed was long and drawn out with an absolute denial of guilt by Gibbs. The police had put together a strong case against him. Numerous letters he had written explaining the absence of this wife over the weeks prior to the body were examined by an expert and in his opinion they had been written by Gibbs. His handwriting sample had been taken in prison by a warder.

One startling observation brought up in the Assize Court was that Gibbs was seen at the Hall wearing the same clothes both on both 12th and 13th May. It was asked in his defence that if the alleged murder of his wife took place on the 12th of May, then why would he wear clothes, covered in blood stains, the following day? It was an interesting point that added to his defence observations that the jury should not be judging on immorality, potential bigamy, or indeed disreputable behaviour – that's as maybe, but it does not prove murder.

Another twist in the case was another death. During the trial at the Monmouthshire Assizes it was brought to the attention of the police of a suicide of a man named John Rogers. He had hanged himself from a tree very close to the location where the body of Mrs Gibbs was found. It seemed very suspicious, a murder and a suicide in the same locale. This occurrence did not seem to be mentioned at all at Gibbs' trial. This came up in police enquiries but did not appear to be pursued. Perhaps a mention of this might have weakened the case against Gibbs.

The defence barrister brought up many inconsistencies as he saw them in the evidence. There was evidence of burning material in the Hall's small incinerator, which the prosecution had claimed was from towels burnt by Gibbs, as though he had used them to clean himself. This allegation was ridiculed by the defence. Many other items of extremely good circumstantial evidence were negated by the defence. Such as, why would he have taken her to a spot within a few yards of the gamekeeper's cottage, the gamekeeper being a man who was supposed to be out all hours of the night, and accompanied by dogs? He would not think of going to such a place to commit murder, but a stranger would go there, because he would not be aware of its proximity to the places he had mentioned.

Gibbs' barrister then stated that the case had not been made out at all, and that the evidence was not of conclusive character which would warrant a jury in sending a man to his death. He insisted that the statements of the witnesses varied greatly. He wound up by asking the jury to give the defendant the benefit ot that doubt which they must in a case of such grave importance.

The trial had been intense, having all forms of evidence presented to the jury. Forensic, police interview statements, exhibits, personal statements from the numerous women involved in the case. The jury were sent out to examine the evidence and came to a conclusion: James Henry Gibbs did murder his wife Susan Gibbs. There was uproar in the court and as soon as the jury foreman spoke, uproar in the square outside as well. The judge brought order to the court.

He donned the black head cloth and spoke:

> *"Charles Gibbs. You have been found guilty of a most diabolical act. Your life is forfeited. Let me implore you not to indulge in any fruitless hopes of endeavour to get a mitigation of your punishment. Of that there is no hope. Let me beg of you to apply your mind to higher considerations. Eternity is before you. Your days are numbered. You will have the instruction and counsel of those who are appointed to give you spiritual help. Seek that mercy and salvation which you cannot expect from any earthly power. Salvation is provided for the worst; and great as your sin is, you are not beyond the reach of that mercy which has been so richly provided. I hope and pray that your mind may be directed to that source from which you may had peace and salvation My province is to pronounce the sentence of death, the only sentence which the law allows me to pass, and that is, that you be taken from hence to the prison from whence you came and then to a place of execution and there hanged by the neck till you are dead and that your body be buried in the precincts of the prison, and, I can only add may you seek and find salvation."*

Gibbs was taken down to the cells sobbing, then away by horse and cart to prison.

Usk Prison was brand new in 1874. Today the small town still has a peaceful and rural feel to it. The River Usk meanders through fields, meadows and woods. The main street and Twyn Square have delightful hostelries and period houses and Usk has the feel as though nothing has changed in over one hundred years. One wonders why in the 1870s anyone would choose Usk as the location of a major prison. It must have been no more than a small village with its Norman castle looking down and its little streets perhaps busy with horse drawn carts. The prison was built virtually in the centre of town. Usk had been the location of a prison in the 18th century and perhaps it seemed that a new prison was a logical expansion.

it was in Usk Prison that James Henry Gibbs spent his last days praying to God. It was noted that his devotion to the Bible led him to quote it incessantly, perhaps in the knowledge that the only redemption he could gain would be from his Maker.

Monday 24th August, 1874, was the day of Gibbs' execution. No other person could describe that awful day in such a graphic manner than a contemporary newspaper journalist. He was with the condemned man from dawn until his demise and reported on his last hours. It is a grim and morbid narrative which is not an easy read.

> *This morning, the last which Gibbs was to see in this world, was one of the most beautiful that had been experienced through a very fine summer. The sun shone with great brilliancy, and were it not that the falling leaves gave indications of autumn, it might have been considered a spring morning. The birds were flying about rapidly, and the groves to the east and west sent out hundreds of songsters, who hovered round the prison, and then perched on the top of the external walls warbling melodiously, while the ghastly preparations for death were going on inside, Scarcely could a more lovely spot be selected for the erection of a gentleman's mansion than that on which the County Gaol for Monmouthshire has been built. The river Usk flows a short distance in front, and then a steep rising ground to the west of the Llanbaddock Road covered with trees. To the east of the*

prison the land rises again, and to the north the town of Usk. The landscape is one of great beauty, the valley of Usk containing some of the finest scenery in the county. But within the walls of the prison, although the sun's rays might penetrate, no glimpse of nature could be seen, and the only life that he could see were the groups of birds fluttering joyously about, a few feet from his cell. The County Gaol at Usk is one of the most modern erections of the kind in the county. The different portions of the prison are enclosed in a high wall, but the angles are rounded to prevent the indentation which time might cause. The entrance is flanked by octagonal towers, with long slits deeply indented in the masonry, protected on the inside by stout glass, through which the warders can command a view of the approach to the outer gate. The towers give the entrance a castellated appearance, but as the walls round are equal in height to the towers, nothing else is visible. A field of pasture land extend on one side and a small avenue leads round to the back. The front entrance leads into a small courtyard, prettily laid out with flowers, but a second wall in which are another pair of massive gates, with a warder on guard behind, obstruct the view of the visitor from the interior of the prison itself. From the time of his condemnation Gibbs has appeared to exhibit peculiar traits. Whatever pressure of anxiety there might be upon his mind, he never gave any outward tokens of it. Up to the last he slept well, and ate and drank well, but last night he was restless. The governor of the gaol, Colonel Millman, went to see him this morning about five o'clock. He was then asleep, I but soon woke up, and the Governor then desired the warders to leave the room. They did so, and the Governor then said 'Gibbs, have you anything to say to me, as this probably is the last time I shall have the opportunity of speaking to you?'

*He said, 'Yes, but all I have to say is, I am still innocent.'
The Governor replied, 'The verdict of all the world is against you, for you have never even satisfied your attorney that you are innocent.'
Gibbs replied, 'God knows that I am innocent.'
At half-past six o'clock the Chaplain, the Rev Mr Cadwallader, then entered the condemned cell and remained praying with Gibbs for half-an-hour. He spoke to the Chaplain in his usual manner, and still protested his innocence.
The Governor of the gaol, knowing his extreme fondness for sausages, had a breakfast of sausages prepared for him. He sent it in by one of the warders, and Gibbs made a hearty breakfast off them.
All this time Gibbs remained in his condemned cell, a light and airy apartment, but he was soon afterwards brought down to a cell adjoining the corridor, which opened into one of the court yards. Here a platform had been constructed on the side of which was the gallows, an old one brought from Monmouth many years since, and only used once that is, about fifteen years since, when Edward Rees was hung for the murder of his wife. The scaffold was painted black, and to enable the flap to be greater than could otherwise be the case, when the scaffold was only three feet from the ground, a pit more than two feet deep was dug.
Soon afterwards he was removed from the condemned cell, and the executioner, William Marwood, of Horncastle, was introduced, and began to pinion him.
At half-past seven the High Sheriff, Mr Crawshay Bailey, arrived at the gaol and also the Under Sheriff, Mr E. B. Edwards. At this time about a dozen persons were loitering outside the gate of the prison, and about a similar number were to be seen about the corners of the streets. No excitement prevailed, and but little interest*

seemed to be manifested in the event.

The surgeon of the gaol, Dr Boulton, the chaplain, and Captain F. Herbert, one of the county magistrates, arrived, and were admitted. At a quarter to eight the representatives of four papers were admitted, and received in the office by the Governor, who conducted them to the magistrates' room, the window of which looked into the prison exercising ground, where the scaffold had been erected. As soon as the Chaplain had entered the task of pinioning the culprit commenced. He seemed up.to this point to preserve a staid and reserved demeanour and walked firmly along the corridor to the cell. It is now he broke down, and when his hands were secured he broke out in yells and groans that were terrible to listen to. A few minutes before eight o'clock the Governor, the High Sheriff, the Under Sheriff, the Sheriff's Officer, Mr Graham, entered the room, and the Governor delivered over the body of Gibbs to the High Sheriff for execution. The funeral service then began. Up to this time Gibbs had been sobbing bitterly, but when the service commenced and the executioner bound his hands, his cries and groans were terrible to listen to, and he writhed in mental agony. Parker, the chief warder, and Honess, the second warder, who had lately been almost constantly with him had to hold him on the chair. The officials of the gaol, and the Governor and the High Sheriff, with Capt Herbert and others, then passed into the court-yard, and as the Chaplain began, 'I am the resurrection and the life,' the mournful procession passed along the passage to the scaffold.

Gibbs was almost carried by the warders. He was quite unable to stand, and was groaning and crying with great agony. He was carried to the scaffold, followed by the executioner. It was one of the most horrible sights to witness Gibbs was held upon the scaffold under the fatal drop by the two warders, while the executioner bound his legs. The Funeral Service could scarcely be heard his groans and cries being so loud when the cap was tied over his head. During this time he was crying 'Lord have mercy upon me, Lord have mercy upon me.'

The Reverend Cadwallader, climbed up the gallows steps and stood in a position to which he had been allocated during the rehearsal the day before. One wonders what a Christian priest thought of the state murder of an individual. It is doubtful that he agreed with the principle and was probably tight-stomached and deeply upset. His sustained reading of Bible passages, which, as a constant backdrop to the scene, probably added to the feeling of melancholy and despondence to all present. Perhaps it may have given succour to Gibbs as a devout Christian and it may have been helpful knowing that a representative of God was present and praying for his soul.

When all the arrangements were completed Gibbs almost screamed, "Oh, for God's sake a moment."

The Governor of the gaol came up to him and said, "Gibbs, what do you want?"

The culprit cried out, "God forgive me for these and all my past sins. He knows that I am innocent, and I am happy that he knows that I am innocent. I die innocent. Lord have mercy upon me."

The Governor says, "Nothing more?"

At the last moment, he cried out, "Good bye my parents, good bye all. Good bye friends, Good bye. May the Almighty have mercy upon me." His groans were pitiful, and he was left on the fatal drop, his knees tottering, his whole frame trembling, and literally hanging by the rope around his neck.

The funeral service continued. *The Lord's Prayer* was said, all present joining in, and in a few moments the drop fell with a crash, and Gibbs fell with a jerk. His struggles were brief, and before the funeral service was ended all was over with him in this world. The bell of the parish church tolled for half an hour before and half an hour after. As soon as it was all over the black flag, inscribed with the word *Justice* in white letters on a black background, was hoisted over the entrance to the gaol. The Governor and the surgeon approached the drop and found that Gibbs was dead.

The coroner held an inquest within a few hours. It must have been a stern duty for the jury to discipline themselves to view the still warm body of James Henry Gibbs. One by one they filed into a cell, not far from the scaffold, where the body had been placed on the wooden bed. It was noted that Gibbs' expression seemed normal in death, as though he had died of natural causes. The body was identified to each juror by the Governor.

Back in the room set aside for the coroner the doctor certified death and a representative of the High Sheriff of Monmouthshire stated that it was a legal happening as Gibbs was lawfully sentenced to death by hanging by a properly constituted court.

It was noted that a letter was received at the prison from Gibbs' father who pleaded with his son to confess his guilt. Gibbs went to his death protesting his innocence.

Once the crowd outside the prison dispersed there seemed to return a sense of normality in the district. The excitement caused by the event disintegrated and life seemingly went back to normal in Usk.

James Henry Gibbs was buried in a plot within the prison walls. Placed at the head of the plot was a cross. Marked on the cross was the numeral '1'.

The death of James Henry Gibbs brought to an end a trial that had gripped the citizens of Cardiff, Monmouth, and Usk. They'd avidly followed the case via news sheets and word of mouth. Many people believed Gibbs was a rogue but not a murderer.

He was dead. The case was over. The judge and jury had done their jobs. He had been dragged screaming to the gallows protesting his innocence. Many felt sorry for James Henry Gibbs whom they classified as a wronged man.

Then a dumbfounding thing took place. Five days after Gibbs' execution a report appeared in the *Cardiff Times* of a conversation between one of their reporters and a Mr Lewis of St Mellons. Lewis was an associate of Gibbs, being in the same Forester's Lodge. He was also a Church Warden and a successful farmer.

Lewis stated he had visited Gibbs in prison and a conversation had taken place about the last time he had seen his wife. Gibbs then told Lewis some startling facts which Lewis had kept to himself as it had been told to him in confidence by Gibbs, Lewis not wanting to break that confidence whilst Gibbs was alive. Now he was dead Lewis thought it worth mentioning. James Henry Gibbs had admitted leaving his wife in a ditch!

Llanrumney fields near the murder scene, photographed in the same decade.

A quick look at the evidence that had come out in the court proceedings show that witnesses saw a woman who they believed to be Susan Gibbs making her way to Llanrumney on the probable night of her murder. She had gone to the top of Penylan Hill where it was said by passing witnesses that she met her husband and then they both wandered down the other side of Penylan Hill towards the little hamlet of Llanedeyrn. The River Rumney would have been crossed via a rickety footbridge, then over a stile onto the footpath to the Hall. Gibbs' protestations of innocence to the facts, together with the accumulation of evidence must have been confusing to the jury.

If only Lewis had told them this!

Gibbs further told him in confidence when they were alone in a prison cell, that he had written to this wife to ask her to come to see him and it was agreed they meet at Penylan. He wanted to talk things through and his intention was to leave her at a cottage that he knew on the Llanrumney Hall estate. She could then walk home, even though late at night. They made their way through some gates towards two cottages talking all the time. Gibbs then told Lewis that he realised that the cottage was not too far from St Mellons and the residence where Mary Ann Jones lived with her parents. (What is known is that the cottage had a stone staircase and a view of Peterstone Church in the far distance.)

Gibbs went on to say that he left Susan in a field hoping she would go back to her lodgings in Cardiff. (By now it must have been dark.) She refused to go back and followed him towards the Hall. Gibbs and his wife started struggling, which turned into a fight that left Susan Gibbs unconscious. Sensationally, he then went on to tell Lewis it was he who placed her unconscious body in a ditch. He returned to Llanrumney Hall. He did not go any further in his narrative than that.

It is a damning indictment, if true, of Gibbs' involvement in his wife's murder.

Lewis put a confidential obligation before a moral obligation.

What probably occurred after the fight was Gibbs returned to the Hall to fetch his cut-throat razor. (He was seen to come in, then go out soon after by other servants.) He would have returned to the unconscious body as fast as he could and, lifting her up, he cut the poor woman's throat and dumped her.

Perhaps it is worth repeating Gibbs' last screams as he stood on the gallows with the rope around his neck:

> *"God forgive me for these and all my past sins. He knows that I am innocent, and I am happy that he knows that I am innocent. I die innocent. Lord have mercy upon me."*

Llanrumney Hall today stands silent witness to one of the most awful and macabre events in its history. Today it could be a house, a shop or a garden, not far from Llanrumney Hall, that is built on the exact spot Susan's body was found decomposing in the hedgerow one and half centuries ago. Records do not show the location and perhaps it is for the best.

CHAPTER SEVEN

Debtors: the painful demise of William Jenkins

Being in debt was a scourge and a serious crime during times past. Each gaol had a wing or section that catered for arrested people charged with offences relating to debt. In London, there were whole establishments dedicated to debt-related offences.

Debtors put behind bars usually hoped and prayed that someone would turn up and pay the debts for them, and thus triggering their release back into society. If one was poor that was highly unlikely but the authorities accepted even paltry amounts of money paid to reduce debt.

There was a difference between debtors and other prisoners. Debtors did not have to do hard labour, such as the treadmill, they were generally let off the savage penal work of the Victorian and Edwardian eras.

The cities, towns, and country were infested with pedlars, hawkers and mongers of domestic items, from knives to pegs. Many unscrupulous mongers left goods on the doorsteps of houses then immediately vacated the area. They returned a few days later to demand payment. If it was not forthcoming the bailiffs were called in, and the occupiers of the house found themselves behind bars until the debt was paid. It is said in one journal that half the people in debtors' prison in 1879 had been victims of this particular swindle.

It seems the responsibilities of investigating and chasing debtors was passed from the police to county bailiffs. Police officers assisted in the event of a potentially fiery situation occurring during an arrest.

An Irishman in Cardiff was arrested by the County Court bailiffs for non-payment of 15/- (75p). He had fallen foul of a hawker who had left drapery at his home without his permission. En route to Cardiff Gaol the man begged the bailiffs to call in at his work to pick up his pay so he could expunge the debt. It had got considerably bigger as costs had been added. His wages were 18/- therefore enough to pay off the outstanding monies owing to the draper. As he was paying over the 15/- he suddenly drew back and held on to his money. He commented that it would only leave him 3/- (15p) to last him the week. He said to the bailiffs, "No, I'll go to gaol." He promptly pocketed the 18/-, refused to pay and was duly marched off to Cardiff Gaol.

It was said in court at a later date that he had not realised that even after being fed an awful diet, and been incarcerated each day in a cell, that on his release he would still owe 15/-, also, that he would be arrested again, which he duly was!

The savagery of the legal system was often criticised by newspapers and many canvassed for a fairer regime. It was the richest echelon of society that pulled the strings and it usually ended with the lower ones paying the price. At some time in our lives we may all get into debt, be it minor or major, be it temporary or permanent, be it a mortgage or paper bill, the money has to be paid back.

Bailiffs are as an important part of civil court life today as they were a hundred years ago. Today there is more understanding and leniency when dealing with a genuine individual who gets into debt. A century ago it was usually the man of the house who was the breadwinner and, generally, he made the fiscal decisions. If he got into debt then legal action was taken against the whole family, including the wife and their children. Back in Victorian times, if there was no money coming into the household or the man was in prison then the family would probably get evicted and end up in the poor house.

A story from the 1890s perhaps sums up the difficulties of the working man and his family's finances. Mr William Jenkins was employed as a 'baller' (a man who divides metal into separate balls), at a South Wales iron works. It was hard, manual work in awful conditions. The searing heat in which he worked six days a week ensured that his clothing was permanently wet with perspiration and his face burnt bright red. He was physically exhausted. Without the pittance he was paid, his family would suffer and eventually be evicted from the house.

Most small terraced houses were supplied by the employer and the rent paid to them. More often than not the wages were paid in tokens which could only be spent at the 'company store', a shop owned, of course, by the employer. Part of the wages would be in cash to settle family debt outside of the company store purchases. William had accrued a small debt purchasing material for clothes for his family. The debt of just £1 and a few pennies was reported to the local bailiff at the county court in Merthyr. The court had made an order for William to pay, but he failed to do so.

Rather than negotiate William's position, a well-known, heartless, and tough bailiff called at the house and waited for William to return home from work. William was arrested and then walked on a cold winter's night to a police station. His clothes were wet with perspiration and he was in no fit state to walk anywhere. He was placed in a freezing cell with no form of heat. It was so cold that the other occupants of the cell lay back to back in an attempt to keep warm. They both complained of the bitter cold to an officer but nothing was done. This resulted in William walking back and forth in the tiny cell all night.

The following morning, he was taken handcuffed by train to Cardiff Gaol and placed in a cell with another debtor. After two more days he was afflicted by periods of severe diarrhoea for which he was medicated by the local doctor.

Two days later William was dead and the Coroner's Court revealed that the cause of death was an infected lung.

Perhaps a local newspaper comment at the time illustrates how society felt about petty debtor's crime.

> *The bailiffs must be taught a moderation in the execution of their orders, and not allowed to drag a man from home like a felon, half dressed and exhausted; to throw him into a dungeon like a street-walker and a drunkard to parade him through the highway handcuffed like a thief.*

The moral crusade continued with the following, poignant statement:

> *...but who amongst us can deny the possibility of becoming poor or going down by degrees to the lowest verge of wretchedness and distress of parting with friend after friend, until we stand alone in the world, unpitied and forlorn, and eventually dying as this man died, like a dog in chains.*

One wonders what happened to William's wife and children but, in all probability they were evicted and admitted to the workhouse. It seems senseless today, as in the long run it would cost more to feed and clothe the family in an institution than it would to have to give William more time to pay his debt. But, the law is the law, of which William Jenkins fell foul in a most catastrophic way.

CHAPTER EIGHT

The short and brutal life of PC John Henry Kingdom

*PC John Henry Kingdom
26'A', Cardiff Borough
Constabulary
b.1869, d.1904*

Engrossing, violent, and tragic are words that sum up the tempestuous career of Constable John Henry Kingdom. It was cut short in dreadful circumstances in the year 1904. He had completed just ten years' service in the Cardiff Borough Constabulary.

Kingdom had served for seven years in the Inniskilling Dragoons and wanted something different, that something was to stay on the front line, this time on the cruel and savage streets of Cardiff. It was the wrong choice. It seems the constant physical attacks, the daily stresses of the 'coal face', and upsetting scenes took their toll on this family man. It was a hard life and he paid with his.

On 16th March, 1894 at the commencement of his police career he was posted to the 'A' Division, which covered the central and docks areas of Cardiff. Until the very last officer patrolled the very last beat in 1969 nothing much had changed. 'A' division was Central Station and Bute Street was the sub-station. The only other official shelter for officers within the division was a small hut at the entrance to the dock gate in Bute Place. The hut survived until 1969 and was known as Pillar 13.

Kingdom found a very different world on the streets of Cardiff from his army career. Each and every day he was fighting, not for his country against an enemy, but for one class against another, or that's how it must have seemed. Rich and powerful gentlemen appointed the law enforcers, including magistrates, court clerks, bailiffs and the police. They were there to keep the lower classes in order and in their place.

Some of the most well to do houses were sometimes side by side with the savage streets. Officers from the central station were ordered to march up and down streets like Charles Street to protect the occupants from any intrusion into their peace. It was only a hundred yards away where the back streets and residential courts housed some of the poorest people, their drinking places, disorderly houses, and their raucous social escapades.

It was extremely rare that officers entered into the rich houses of Llandaff, North Road, Newport Road, or Charles Street. The supervisory sergeants and constables knew their place. It was the occupants of these rich houses who would be sitting on the benches as magistrates or mixing in the social circles of the influential families. Kingdom was well-aware of his responsibilities and his position in life. His was to keep law and order on the streets and that in itself was a frightening prospect for anyone, let alone a new recruit.

Two weeks prior to Christmas 1894, very early in his service, he was sent to investigate reports of fighting in the entrance to the central market. He was new in the job and perhaps had not realised that Christmas was one of the most violent times of the year – mostly caused by alcohol. He was attacked by numerous men. It was brutal in the extreme and there were concerns for the life of Kingdom. He left hospital and was sent home and it was only on Christmas Day that he managed to leave his bed for an hour. On Boxing Day, he managed two hours out of bed.

He gradually gained strength and, to the surprise of his doctors and indeed his wife, he was back to work two weeks later. The men who attacked John Henry Kingdom were never caught. It was more than likely they were mariners and in town enjoying the delights of Cardiff life before departing on a ship bound who knows where.

Life was never boring in Victorian Cardiff. Kingdom always involved in some sort of incident from rescuing a woman who had jumped in the Taff to beating down the doors of the many shebeens (illegal drinking dens) that had been set up in the centre of the town. The usual place for these criminals was around Bridge Street and Mary Ann Street. Kingdom was often ordered by his Sergeant to slip on a civilian jacket, or come to work in plain clothes, and keep watch on a certain premises. The usual period of observation was fifteen minutes. If it was an active shebeen that's all it would take to gain enough evidence to force an entry. Of course, it was not a job that Kingdom could do alone. He had to have a fellow officer at the rear door to catch miscreants making good their escape.

Constable Kingdom must have wondered at first why, with 131 licensed pubs and alehouses in the centre of Cardiff, anybody would bother to enter a shebeen to buy alcohol. Well the answer was simple – it was cheaper. Illegal brew-houses with no normal overheads could do a roaring trade until they got caught and closed down. Kingdom would know the problems that alcohol and drunkenness brought to the streets so anything he could do stop it he would.

Christmas Day brought no comfort to Kingdom, no time of peace. Another Christmas, another incident. He was violently assaulted in Bridge Street by drunken men, not far from the shebeen he had forcibly entered. The men, who had completely lost control of themselves in a drunken rage, turned on the lone officer. He managed to blow his whistle and within a minute help arrived. The drunken, fighting men were dragged to the police station in St Mary Street. That was no mean feat as any 1960s officer would tell you: hanging onto aggressive prisoners was difficult and it was self-defence that sometimes calmed them down. The men were sent to prison for one month.

And so life went on for the officer dealing with the worst that human nature could throw at him.

Thomas Davies was released from Cardiff Gaol at 8.00am. By lunchtime he was fighting with the police and causing a major disturbance, once again in Bridge Street. With the plethora of drinking establishments in the area getting drunk was no problem. It was on the corner of Mary Ann Street and Bridge Street that a large crowd had gathered to see this boisterous, snarling, and scary man cause havoc. One shopkeeper had chased him out of his premises but Davies had turned around and was shadow boxing with him.

On hearing the commotion and then seeing the event, Constable Kingdom must have thought, "Here we go again. It's going to be one of those days." Hell on the streets was usually more apparent during the late afternoons, evenings, and the night time. The problem with large crowds is that they can very easily turn on you, or make life difficult to diffuse a situation as they are enjoying the spectacle. Some are fuelled by alcohol themselves, and it doesn't take much encouragement for them to join in as well.

Kingdom told Davies to be quiet and leave, it obviously did not work as he ran at the officer and attempted to punch and kick him. Davies was verbally and physically aggressive and the alcohol had knocked any sense out of him. Kingdom dragged the man along Bridge Street in the direction of the Waterloo Bridge with him kicking, spitting, and punching. No doubt the crowd followed. But it was Kingdom who was in charge and with a hold around the other man's neck he dragged him to St Mary Street Police Station. No doubt on the way a calming punch or two had to be administered.

No sooner had Kingdom returned to Bridge Street than he was in trouble again. More fighting! This time it took three officers and the use of a horse drawn cab to get the man to the Town Hall police station.

Both had a string of convictions for violence and crime. Both men were either fined at the following morning's court or suffered a month in prison.

Women were not given much respect by men at the time, if the newspapers are anything to go by. It appears they were categorised as second-class citizens by many in Victorian society. Of course, this may be a generalisation but it seems to be true when examining the facts. The suffrage movement was still decades away and a woman's place was mostly in the home.

In the impoverished areas of central Cardiff and the docks, women were thought of even less of. The brothels and street prostitution put women in a very poor light, but for the majority of these girls and women it was the only way they could earn any money. In fact, many husbands insisted their wives worked the streets in times of financial hardship. Kingdom would have seen women leaving their homes at times corresponding with the channel tides and waiting for ships to parade their wares on the dockside, and then returning to their homes in the company of a paying client or clients.

This lack of respect brought other problems for Kingdom and his colleagues. Men, mostly drunk, would accost women walking along the streets and try to kiss them. This was a usual event and the common response was the woman either hitting them with their handbag or fist, or calling the police if there was one nearby – and in those days, there usually was. The breach of the peace offences came from 14th century common law. If it was just after the event, the 1861 Offences Against the Persons Act gave an officer a multitude of powers.

Kingdom could arrest someone if he heard a suspect use obscene language, and that is the offence the man would be charged with. The problem with women though, hardened by street life, is that they acted in a most capricious manner. Kingdom was escorting a semi-drunk woman one evening to her home in Butetown and walking alongside her. He knew her, she was pleasant when sober but a little unpredictable when in drink. She seemed appreciative of the security but for some reason she turned aggressive, totally out of the blue. She suddenly attempted to push her hat pin into the officer's eye! His quick movement led to the pin missing the eye but penetrating his nostrils side-on. With the pin sticking out of his nose he got the woman to her house then made his way as fast as he could to the police station in Bute Street where he sat down and slowly drew the hat pin out of his nose. Neat whisky was no doubt used to clean up the tiny, but intrusive wound. It can be imagined that station banter was rife, with the comedians in the station having a field day. In truth though it was a very serious incident that could have led to the officer being blinded in one eye, or worse. It would have taught Kingdom and his fellows to perhaps not be as helpful in the future and to be very wary of semi-intoxicated women.

A few days later the well-known, (in the local station), Sarah Weeks was playing up in Bute Street. She was told to be quiet and go home, but she refused. She attacked Kingdom, kicking and punching him. As usual the woman was dragged to Bute Street Police Station and pushed into a cell. They were situated at the back left of the building as you walked in and the screams of the inhabitants could be heard all around the ground floor including the public enquiry office. There had been a door to the cell block in Kingdom's day but it had been removed many years later. Weeks appeared in court and was sent to prison for 14 days hard labour. She had only just come out. For some people, this was their way of life, and there was no shame or ignominy in being arrested or imprisoned.

* * *

Kingdom, Hinge, and a third officer, receiving an award.

Kingdom mounted on a horse, likely rented from a nearby trader.

John Henry Kingdom was a professional cavalryman, therefore his services were often called upon during demonstrations and VIP events, including Royal visits. It is known that between the two world wars horses were rented from Fry's Butchers of Cardiff. They had their own stables as did numerous Cardiff businesses. One would imagine that it was similar a few decades earlier when Kingdom patrolled Cardiff's streets. Kingdom, according to research, always used the same horse, his favourite. In Kingdom's time the saddles were highly polished and one can imagine John Henry proudly working to make sure his steed and saddlery were in perfect ceremonial condition.

It is known that the Cardiff City Police saddles were stored in a disused cell block, on the first floor directly above the old Cardiff City Cell Block in the Law courts. It ran off the Police Parade Room, now a Crown Court. There were up to a dozen saddles stored in this location.

However, one officer who joined the constabulary in the 1940s stated that at that time horses were not rented and he cannot remember there being any police horses in use. Many of the saddles still *in situ* in the 1960s storerooms simply rotted away and were destroyed.

There were quiet days, but not very often. His period in the Cardiff Borough Police was probably the busiest of all in the history of the constabulary. It was not only violence aimed at the officers on the streets, they also had to attend to the results of violence within families and the after-effects of street fights.

The morgue, situated at the rear of Bute Street Police Station, became a second home for many officers as they deposited the bodies of men, women, and children who had died not only by natural causes, but by disease, starvation, drowning, neglect, and violence.

The police station in Bute Street must have been an oasis where Kingdom could perhaps play cards, drink a cup of tea, watch the kettle simmering on the coal fire or simply do his paperwork with a pen and nib dipped into pots of ink. Kingdom's world did not change much for the officers who followed for many decades afterwards. It was that kind of police station.

Kingdom found himself in involved as a police witness in a scurrilous case heard at the Cardiff police court on 26th September, 1903. It captured the attention of the public to such a degree that the public galleries were packed.

David John Hughes was 28 years of age and had been married for two years. He was originally a collier and the marriage had taken place in Merthyr Tydfil. The problems for his wife started when they moved to Lewis Street in Canton. Elizabeth was a woman '...of small stature and bashful.' Her coyness was no help, as he beat her regularly. She was of such a quiet demeanour that she took no action against her husband.

She was shocked when he suggested another way of getting money into the home, that she should sell her body! She refused but David had a very strong and overbearing nature. Mr and Mrs Hughes had a lodger, which was normal at the time. The gentleman resided in a single room, caused no trouble, and paid his rent promptly. When they were all together one evening Hughes asked the lodger if he wanted to sleep with his wife. He went on to say he could 'have her' once a week with a just little bit extra being added to his rent. Elizabeth initially refused but pressure was put on her so she succumbed and once a week Hughes slept downstairs.

There then followed more pressure on the woman and it was not long before she was bringing men back to Lewis Street and handing over her takings to her husband. He had a list of ships that were docking in Cardiff and told her to go and meet the ship and parade up and down to attract sex-starved sailors.

Mrs Hughes could take no more and one day she ran into a neighbour's house for help. David chased her and attempted to stab her with a knife, and he would have succeeded if not for the quick thinking of the neighbour, Mrs Saddler. She shouted and he dropped the knife, but she had seen Hughes attempt to injure his wife before by stamping on her.

It was Kingdom, with two others, who undertook the

investigation into the case and interviewed the witnesses. He took his seat in court after giving evidence and waited for the verdict. Did David Hughes live off the immoral earnings of his wife? Kingdom must have been overjoyed, but he showed no emotion, when the magistrate sentenced David Hughes to three months hard labour. The last words of Hughes before he was sent down were, "I am no sanguinary pimp." An adjective which seems long gone from daily use. It means to cause bloodshed. Did that mean that he seemed to think his crimes were of less consequence just because there was no blood?

There was to be one major event that was pivotal in John Henry Kingdom's life, and indeed his death. He was called to attend a disturbance at *The Packet Hotel*, near the main Bute Docks gate. *The Packet* survives and is still open today, the last of scores of pubs that used to populate Bute Street.

Looking out of the windows of the Packet Hotel, 2017.

A drunken Norwegian sailor was refusing to leave the premises and had become threatening to the staff and their customers. PC Kingdom tried to escort him outside but the sailor would only leave on the understanding that the police officer would have a fist fight with him outside in the street. It appears Kingdom felt it best to agree to get him out of the pub, with a view no doubt to then get him back to his ship. Both men walked out into the street and a number of other sailors and locals following to see what would happen. The sailor jumped on the back of the officer and succeeded in pushing him to the ground. After a struggle, Kingdom got the better of the man and dragged him to the main dock gate. He handed him into the charge of the docks police, who took him back to his ship.

The following morning the sailor turned up at Bute Street Police Station and claimed that his gold ring had been lost during the fracas. He even claimed that Kingdom, or another officer, may have stolen it! Police checks found that no ring had been handed in. The sailor left the station and went back to his ship to sail on the next tide, probably, never to return.

However, the story of the ring did not end there.

It was at 52, Pen y Peel Road, Canton that PC Kingdom died. The date was Christmas Day, December 25th, 1904. The reason for his death, a heart attack. This was a few days after rescuing a woman from a burning building on the night of 20th December and carrying her to safety. He was 35 years of age. It makes one think that the rescue was a stress too far, his life was so full of trouble and violence that it had simply got too much for him. His body could take no more and it gave out.

The funeral was a grand affair and many of the local police forces were represented. This included the Glamorgan Police, the Cardiff Railway Police, and the Glamorgan Yeomanry. The Chief Constable, Mr McKenzie, took charge of the parade. He was mounted on a fine horse, and it was John Henry Kingdom's favourite horse, that led the procession. It was exquisitely decked out with black plumes, stirrups turned backwards, the usual funereal attachments, and led by two of Kingdom's comrades.

A strange thing then happened, which seemingly showed the reverence in which Kingdom was held. The incident in *The Packet* had occurred a short time before his untimely death. At the funeral procession his wife was sought out by a man who paid his respects to her. He then handed her a gold ring, saying words to the effect, 'I found this down the Packet pub. I want you to have it. May help if you're short of money.' He then left. Who he was is not known.

A few weeks later, and after all the commotion had died down, his widow, Annie Louise Kingdom, took the ring to a senior officer and told him what had happened. He made enquiries and ultimately returned the ring to her saying she could keep it.

The story and the ring have been passed down through the generations of the Kingdom family. It is a moving memory of a

The descendants of police officers, Hinge and Kingdom, (left), united over 100 years after their great-grandfathers served together, and outside the pub where a gold ring mysteriously disappeared.

Pictured outside The Packet *is the last pub remaining on Bute Street from those days, and the location of the fight between the Scandinavian sailor and Constable Kingdom.*

time when Cardiff life was tough, really tough, especially for Cardiff Borough police officers on front line duties in the town's violent and unpredictable docklands.

However, the story still does not end there. Annie Louise Kingdom and her three small children were soon to be evicted from the police house as her deceased husband's pension was far too small following a mere ten years of police service. Fellow officers made a collection which raised a good sum to help Annie, but she needed to work regularly. She tried to get jobs, she pleaded with the Chief Constable Mr McKenzie at his Cathedral Road home for a job but to no avail. Without regular work the prospects for Annie, and her children, were either prostitution, petty crime, or the workhouse.

Luckily for her just as the thought of the workhouse was permeating her mind a job opportunity arose. The council had just completed the Public Conveniences on the Hayes, (which are still there today), and she found employ as a humble lavatory attendant. This job was the beginning of a new life for her as the bills were being paid and the children had some schooling. She stayed in the job for fifteen years. Everyone in the late officer's family worked together to allow her to satisfy her job needs.

When the children finished each school day at Radnor Road School they walked into town and to the Hayes. They used to stamp up and down on the glass tiles that formed the pavement at street level and the roof of the toilets below, and if the coast was clear they would go down to their mother in her office where they would eat sandwiches and pass the time until her shift finished. At the end of her day police constables often walked the family home for their safety, beat officers passing her from one to the other as she made her way back to Pen-y-Peel Road.

Annie Louise was so industrious with her money, and her caring maternal side so generous, that all three children became successful in life, which in those days meant that they worked and could support themselves. Her youngest son, Ernest, became a much-respected Cardiff Councillor for Canton and a city

Alderman. As leader of the Labour Party he was next in line to be the Lord Mayor of Cardiff, when he unfortunately died in 1965. A civic funeral was held, with the city mace covered in black cloth, and many local dignitaries were in attendance.

By the time she passed away in 1922 at the young age of 47, worn out by hard work and responsibility, all three of Annie's boys were in gainful employment and becoming pillars of the Cardiff community.

The legacy of John Henry Kingdom and Annie Louise continues to live on in their grandchildren. John Kingdom was a lecturer at Sheffield Hallam University and his brother Bob is an actor and writer, best known for his show *Dylan Thomas – Return Journey*, directed by Anthony Hopkins. Ernest's grandson David Thomas recently retired as a respected Mid-Glamorgan head teacher and still lives in Cardiff.

PC John Henry Kingdom would surely have been proud of his wife's struggles to bring up their sons after his death, and then of how successful they became in later life.

Amazingly, the gold ring was never pawned or sold, instead it was been passed down from generation to generation and is still in the family's possession today. An extremely rare and poignant memory of Cardiff's cruel and savage streets and the awful death of their Great Grandfather, Constable John Henry Kingdom.

The gold ring (above), passed down through the generations. A symbol of a brave and determined mother whose traits of resilience and leadership also passed down the family. Being examined (below) by Mark Hinge, Dai Thomas, and Paul Hinge, descendants of constables Hinge and Kingdom.

CHAPTER NINE

Hard times for women – baby abandonment and murder

One has to imagine a baby girl being born into a two-up, two-down terraced home in the predominantly working class areas of the south of Cardiff. The father would have been making a living in the industrial docklands areas or indeed be a sailor and away for long periods. His mother would probably have been busy at home bringing up the other children; cleaning, fetching coal, shopping, supplying meals, washing clothes using a mangle; and involved in the daily battle of just surviving.

The only lighting in the dark houses would be either paraffin or oil, the only heating fuel, coal or wood scavenged in the area or from the docksides. Bedtime would be by candlelight alone. It would have been a hard life and a decent so-called God-fearing family in those days wanted their children to work as soon as possible. School for them was probably a local Board school. There were many such schools in Cardiff, at least one in each suburb. Board Schools were the first State-run centres of learning and administered by a School Board.

If the mother could get a cleaning job herself, or in the parlance of the time, charring, she would jump at the opportunity. Every penny helped to get the children an occasional treat other than essentials.

On Sunday it was imperative, whether Anglican, Catholic, or Non-Conformist, for the family to attend church. For this there had to be a Sunday-best outfit. Everyone tried to be smart, yet one can imagine in a class-based society the differences in what must have been deemed 'Sunday best' must have been wide.

The scene is therefore set for the daughter of the house to obtain work as soon as she could. Being unskilled, other than being a hard worker, the most obvious employment was to go into service as a domestic.

It did not take long for the new middle class families to realise the manual work in the home could be easily outsourced to domestic assistants, servant girls. There were hundreds available, and nearly all of them were hard working, humble individuals desperate for a job. The most attractive asset to a would-be employer, the wages. Cheap, very cheap!

Today we may hope to get a job and try desperately hard to achieve it with no qualifications or proper schooling. It is doubtful we would have to *beg* for employment. Not so then! Begging for a job was not unusual. This might involve promises to work every hour of the day, and put the employer's family first. Or exhibit complete willingness to please the family, your employer..

Then comes another side of servitude, dealing with the master, his family, and his friends. An attractive female servant must have been the target of many men, especially if they could wield power or influence. This may not have been in the employer's home, there could have been influences working outside as well. Young men with the 'Marry me and I'll get you away from all this,' approach. It may sound simplistic, but in examining the reasons for baby abandonment the answers sometimes may be that easy.

Women were vulnerable where the act of sexual intercourse was sometimes an act of compliance, with no real comprehension of the potential consequences. Those consequences sometimes led to the most awful scenarios. Thousands ended up in workhouses and ultimately many in paupers' graves.

With no adequate method of contraception, pregnancy would have been an unsurprising outcome of a casual sexual encounter, whether forced, reluctantly allowed, or wanted. The father of the child, if not admitted, would have been impossible to prove. The girl would be branded a 'whore' and worse. These were hard times.

It was not until 1922 that the Infanticide Act was introduced giving a defence to a mother who murdered a newborn child, if it could be proved that the balance of her mind was disturbed as a result of that birth. Therefore, in such cases there was no mandatory death sentence and it gave judges the power to reduce the sentence to a manslaughter charge with its less severe sentencing options. Acts were constantly being amended and updated.

THE DINGLE DEATH

At the centre of this case is a small area of wooded land in Penarth known as The Dingle. The Dingle is still there, in the form of a very pleasant park, ably looked after by the community and residents who promote its use as a recreational area.

Emily Culliford was born in Penarth in 1875 and baptised in the town on 25th August. Her mother died in 1889, and her father four years later in 1893. She was just sixteen years of age in 1891 when, like many of her class, she went into service as a domestic (a euphemism for being virtually a slave). What happened to her in the following three years scarred her for life.

It is known by research that young servant girls, (especially the attractive ones, as Emily was said to be), were vulnerable to men, both in work and outside. It was not unusual for young vulnerable women to be overpowered emotionally and physically – resulting in an unwanted pregnancy. This was the era of the 'baby farmers', who bought newborn babies from shamed mothers. The era of young, unmarried girls being put on the streets for bringing shame on themselves and their family. This was an era for unwanted newborns being abandoned as it was another mouth to feed. It was an all too common occurrence for the police to be called to the scene of yet another abandonment of a newborn baby. The deaths of these children was usually caused by starvation or physical attack.

The modern entrance to Dingle Park, 2017.

Emily had worked for just a couple of employers in her life, one of which was Mrs Martha Green of Cowbridge Road in Cardiff. She had worked for Mrs Green for over a year and she was said to be reliable, clean, and very reserved. Another descriptive term to describe Emily was that she was modest.

Emily's last surviving close relative, her father, died whilst she was in the service of Mrs Green. It was noted by Mr and Mrs Green that his death hit Emily hard, and she complained of being unwell on several occasions.

Emily left the employment of the Greens to enter into service in Glebe Street, Penarth. Emily had been brought up in Penarth. The Parkers, who had taken Emily into their employ on March 18th, were known to Emily. Mrs Parker had known Emily since she was a small girl so when she heard that she was coming home to Penarth for her health's sake she welcomed her into her home as a domestic. She knew Emily to be a gentle and caring girl who was not a person to go out at night or drink alcohol. Therefore, we are getting a picture of Emily as a kind, caring and mild individual, one to be nurtured in any employment as reliable and trustworthy.

Emily had gone to live with her sister, Mrs Screen, not far from Glebe Street. Mr Screen worked at the local docks in Penarth, again a short distance from their home. Things were about to get bad for Emily as she was soon to be the principal in a murder enquiry!

Young Arthur Wellington of Harriett Street, Cogan, Penarth was out one morning in early 1894 collecting sticks in the Dingle. His father had ordered him to do so and this was a regular occurrence for him. To light the fires in the family home required kindling and the woods was full of it. Arthur saw a brown paper parcel not far from the road. It appeared well secured, so rather than touch it he decided to walk home and tell his father about his find.

Walter, Arthur's father, went with his son to the park and was shown the parcel. He opened it and, to his horror, he saw the body of newborn baby boy. Around its neck was a string pulled tightly. The baby was wrapped in part in what appeared to be a nightdress. He told his son to quickly get to the nearby police station and tell an officer.

He soon told the police that the parcel had not been there a few days ago, and appeared dry. It was noted that it had rained the night before so the parcel could not have been *in situ* long. Arthur told the police that he had been collecting sticks for about 45 minutes and he noticed no-one else in the park, but he did see a man on the adjacent road. He also said that there did not appear to be any disturbance of the long grass and nettles around the package.

An officer then went to the park and viewed the body of the baby. He reacted by sending for other officers and his superior officer, Inspector Rutter.

Some hours later Inspector Rutter made his way to the Dingle to examine the awful find. He noted that the baby had a tight band secured around its neck, so tight that to all present it was the obvious cause of the death. The body was wrapped in a nightdress, which he examined. It was marked at the bottom *Emily Culliford*.

The police couldn't believe their luck. The era before DNA identification meant it could have been a long haul to find the mother of the baby. In many cases neither the mother nor father was ever traced, so many such deaths remained unresolved. Arthur Wellington had a nodding acquaintance with Emily Culliford and he informed the inspector of who Emily was. Everything was going right for Inspector Rutter. He didn't even have to try and trace Emily, the witness who found the body knew where she lived! It was an open and shut case.

Mrs Screen, Emily's sister, told the investigating officers that a rag and bone man had called three times a week to Penarth and she had seen him dealing with Emily on a few occasions. She also said that she had noticed Emily getting a little stout but that was put down to her feeling unwell.

Mrs Stokes of Glebe Street told the police that she had been in Mrs Screen's home and that her sister (Emily) was present. This was about a month previously and she too noticed that Emily was putting on weight on her tummy. She had made a rather cutting remark to Emily, "I suppose you have come home to get rid of it, but you will not!"

She noticed a few weeks later that Emily had lost some of that weight and was much slimmer.

Later she admitted that she was on bad terms with Mrs Screen and she made the remark in a temper. In fact, she had said the same thing to Mrs Screen some time before too. There seemed to be nasty little remarks going back and forth between the two and this friction would have lessened the effect of any testimony being produced to a subsequent court hearing.

Dr J Rees of Herbert Terrace, Penarth stated that the conclusion of his post-mortem examination was strangulation. The item used was a linen band.

When Inspector Rutter asked Emily how her nightdress could have been found wrapped around a dead baby she explained she had sold it to a rag and bone man.

Now the open and shut case presented to Inspector Rutter was proving a little more curious than he had initially thought. Everyone spoke highly of Emily and her employers wanted her back and would offer her a job immediately. Emily was known not go out at night and was teetotal.

The other evidence against her was weak. To put on a little weight in that era whilst ill was not unusual, a doctor had confirmed that fact to the police. Another problem was of course who was the father if it was her baby. She would not answer the question as to do so would incriminate her, alternatively she had not been pregnant, so there would have been no father in the case anyway.

In those days, a police officer would have walked through or past the Dingle once every hour or so during the night. All were interviewed but they saw nothing. It is not known if Emily was examined by the doctor, which would surely have added a prime piece of evidence. It is not known if the rag and bone man was interviewed either. What we do know is that Emily appeared at the Barry Dock Police Court and it was found there was enough evidence to send her for trial at Swansea Assizes.

It is fascinating that during the court enquiry Inspector Rutter had publicly commented that he felt very sorry for Emily and considered that she was a decent young lady. A truly bizarre comment in the circumstances but surely one that was not taken into consideration by the coroner as he committed her.

What followed was a cause of complaint in Emily's later court appearances. Whilst in prison on remand she was treated badly and violently by staff and fellow prisoners. She was abused verbally as a murderer and put through some extremely harsh experiences. This did not stop at her initial custodial period.

There was criticism of the authorities in making Emily travel on public transport to get to the court at a busy time, then walk her from station to courtroom thereby incurring the wrath, hatred, and spite of large crowds.

It was women's groups and their individual leaders who were campaigning for a more humane approach to un-convicted female prisoners, especially in domestic crimes such as Emily's.

In Glebe Street there was an ironmonger's shop run by a man called Mayne. He was so angry at Emily's arrest that he started a fund to obtain quality legal assistance for the girl. All monies donated would be acknowledged in writing and passed to Emily. It seemed therefore that the people from Penarth who knew Emily were all for her, it was the ones who did not know her who were the antagonists.

On 25th June, 1894 Emily Culliford stood in the dock at the Swansea Assize Court charged with the offence of child murder. It was a short appearance. The judge, via the jury, after examining the evidence and in consultation with prosecuting authorities threw out the charge. There simply was no compelling evidence to prove, or even suggest, that the baby found at the Dingle woods was Emily's. She was free to go.

It seemed the whole public attitude to Emily's predicament had changed. When she arrived back in Penarth in the early evening she was greeted by hundreds of cheering people, nearly all women. On seeing the horse cab arrive at her home the crowd surged forward, showering Emily with good wishes, clapping, shouting, and cheering. It is said she was carried into the house by neighbours. It is not clear how Emily would have taken this acclaim or whether she would have wanted it. Perhaps it was the neighbourhood's chance to celebrate the undoing of a miscarriage of justice, or showing regret at their initial derogatory behaviour.

The matter was then brought up by Members of Parliament to the Home Secretary as well as in letters delivered from the public who had been appalled at the charges put against Emily. Many knew her to be a quiet, respectable young lady.

Gertrude Genner of Wenvoe Castle was at the forefront of attempting to find money for Emily from a parliamentary fund. She had strong backing from several Welsh MPs. Her main thrust was that the girl should never have been charged, (as stated by numerous legal experts at the time), and that the treatment of un-convicted women up to a trial was degrading and uncivilised. She also questioned why the girl was remanded in custody when so many people were willing to take her in or stand bail for her.

Her plea to the Home Office in London fell on deaf ears. There was no fund. Gertrude Genner was seen a few months later at the Cardiff Horse Fair with a collection box. If the establishment would not help, she would do it herself!

It appears that Emily Culliford then moved to Somerset and married William Henry Gallop in 1896. He was two years younger than her. They moved to Weston Super Mare. A census showed there was a male son called William Mackintosh and that he was born in Scotland. It is not clear who was the parent, Emily or William. William Gallup was not a poor man and was in receipt of a private income. Sadly, he passed away at the age of 29 years in 1906.

At this stage it gets confusing, as it appears that a few months prior to William's death Emily had given birth to a daughter named Gwyneth Cribb. Had she left William and moved on? In June, 1907 she gave birth to another son, Mervyn Clifford Cribb. Both births were registered in the name of Cribb with mother's maiden name shown as Culliford. It seems she married Albert Cribb in 1908. Albert died in Weston Super Mare in 1948 and Emily in the same town four years later in 1952.

It is difficult to comprehend what a woman charged with the murder of her own child goes through and how the event must change her whole life. If the above facts are correct she quickly moved away from the Penarth area and severed all ties. Her domestic life thereafter seemed quite complex, especially in regard to her relationships.

One must not forget that she was described by all as a gentle and modest young lady, reliable and mild in temperament, therefore she must have been a very appealing belle at the time.

If it was not Emily's baby in Dingle wood in 1894. whose was it? All we know is that another young life was taken away at birth. While on this occasion the police thought they had their murderer, they had not. Emily was an innocent girl charged with a heinous crime. They closed the case soon after the Assize verdict and it lay on file. The case papers were filed under *Pending*, then years later it moved to *Murder. Unsolved*.

THE HARROWING STORY OF THE GRANGETOWN SERVANT GIRL

In November 1906 the Stipendiary Magistrate at Cardiff Police Court had standing in the dock in front of him a manifestly unwell young woman. She was held by two officers, her complexion pale, her manner unnerving. She was visibly shaking.

Maud Benson, aged 24, was arrested some three weeks earlier but was so ill she could not be brought before the Stipendiary until now. She had been resident in the workhouse infirmary since her arrest on a charge of the murder of a newborn child, her child.

Maud Alice Benson was born in Cardiff in the early 1880s and was one of at least eight children born to Edwin Benson (born in Cardiff, 1841), and Annie Stoyle (born in Jersey, 1847). Maud's father, Edwin, was a shipwright by trade and worked at Cardiff docks. Maud was just three years old when her mother passed away. As a teenager she is recorded as working at various Cardiff addresses including 62 Mackintosh Place and 54 Neville Street.

Maud is another sad case of a woman becoming pregnant whilst working in the capacity of a domestic servant. In Maud's case she worked for a family in Fitzhamon Embankment. She had to work, she already had an illegitimate child some years before. There is hardly anything known of the circumstances of that birth but one suspects with her gentle and humble persona it may not have been an act of love at the time she conceived.

Maud worked hard, usually seven days a week in the Fitzhamon Embankment house. One of the other domestics in the house noticed Maud was becoming overweight and challenged her about being pregnant, to which Maud replied she was not. She had a cold. Others started to question her and it got around certain parts of Canton that a servant girl was pregnant but denying it. She was being constantly questioned.

As her condition became more apparent she became weaker and that reflected in her work. She *was* pregnant but wanted no-one to know, either because of the embarrassment or much more likely, she would lose her job and therefore her income. She often fell in the house and the garden, which did not help her condition or her state of mind. She was attempting to work as she did prior to her pregnancy to prove her claim that nothing was wrong.

One early evening she stumbled down the stairs in the house, which appeared to bring on contractions. Maud picked herself up and made her way out into Fitzhamon Embankment and walked into the lanes near Neville Street. Her condition was getting worse and she was extremely troubled. She found a quiet place in one of the lanes behind Beauchamp Street and lay down on the muddy surface. There she gave birth to a baby girl. In her panic and distress she tore off the umbilical cord leaving most of it attached to the baby. She was in pain and stumbled around trying to find some relief in movement. She tried to do something with the child but only achieved in getting it covered in dirt and mud and damaged it even more. Maud thought that the baby was stillborn and abandoned it. She went back into her employer's home at around 10.30pm.

It is hard to imagine what state she was in – exhausted, dishevelled, dirty, and confused, she collapsed on the bed. When she awoke she was in intense discomfort, so much so as to force her eventually into the care of the workhouse infirmary where she was given a bed.

After the baby's body was discovered a police investigation would appear to have been an easy one. There was no secret in the area that a servant girl was believed to be pregnant. It was noticed that the appearance of pregnancy had disappeared in Maud coinciding precisely with the discovery of the dead baby in the lane. Maud was arrested by local officers on a charge of the suspected murder of her own child.

Always a debate in a court of law, relating to a case such as Maud's: did the baby have an independent life outside of its mother? The Stipendiary Magistrate asked the experts. The answer was that it *could* have breathed for a couple of seconds on its own, or even a minute before life was extinct, but it could not be completely proven.

Maud was charged with murder. The Stipendiary decided that, in his view, there was no evidence to prove murder and reduced the charge to 'concealment of birth'. Maud was committed to the Assize Court in Swansea, where the judge ordered that there was no case to answer as she had given birth and walked away with no attempt to conceal.

Maud was helped from the dock into the arms of her sister-in-law who had offered to take care of her. They left the court together. Maud had been through her own hell, both physically, mentally and emotionally and once again a question remains: who was the father? It is doubtful if anyone asked, or indeed cared, and nothing came up during research to show any evidence that this question had formally arisen.

In 1918, Maud Benson married Daniel Larcombe in Cardiff. An Alice Maud Larcombe was resident at Whitchurch Mental

Hospital in 1939 and died in Cardiff in 1957.

Maud's case was one whereby the facts of the case and the demeanour of the defendant led to an outcome that was positive. This was unusual as poor girls in Maud's position usually were given short shrift by the courts and the public. The mental and physical torture endured by Maud in those hard times was terrible. It must have changed her for life. The outcome of other such cases was not so positive as Maud's.

A typical newspaper illustration of a reported baby abandonment case.

THE ROATH MURDER, HELEN STREET

The year is 1902 and another harrowing case is to be heard at the Assize Court relating to the murder of a child. This time it was a six-week-old girl. On this occasion though it was not the mother of the baby who was on trial. It was the grandmother.

Annie Lewis was a young woman who lived with her mother, Hannah, and sister, Agnes, at Helen Street, Cardiff. Her father had died many years previously. Their house in Helen Street wasn't owned by Hannah and they lived in two apartments. That rather grand title simply meant two rooms and a shared back scullery alongside the house owner.

Annie met and married Emmanuel Turvey and they lived for some time with her mother in cramped conditions in Helen Street. They had two children but soon after the second was born, problems in the marriage led to Emmanuel leaving his wife and children.

Their home at Helen Street was now in severe financial difficulties and Annie went out to work as a charwoman seven days a week to earn enough to cover their expenses. She worked 14 hours a day, 7 days a week, for 1/6d per day, a low wage even in those days.

Helen Street, a typical terraced road in Cardiff, where Hannah Lewis lived, and was accused of murder.

We do not know who the father was, and once again it is not mentioned in any sources, but Annie fell pregnant again. Perhaps she, like thousands of other women at the time, had sold her body to gain a little extra money simply in order to survive. We shall never know if that was a factor in Annie's case, it certainly wasn't mentioned in court reporting, and it is perhaps an injustice to her to suggest it. The last thing she must have wanted in her financial position was another baby.

Being pregnant meant towards the end of the term she could not work and so the money dried up. On the 18th November, 1901

Annie entered the workhouse as she was destitute and unable to care for herself. A female baby entered the world on 9th December. A workhouse was not the ideal place to keep a baby but there were charitable medical facilities available, as well as assistance from the local Borough. This help came with strict rules and regulations.

Annie was keen to get her baby away from the workhouse to enable her to work again. It was arranged with her mother that she should look after her new baby girl for a weekly fee of 1/6d.

Annie's mother, Hannah Lewis, was not young and was said to be in her early 70s. In those days, that age was deemed very old and few people reached three score years and ten. Indeed she looked older than her years and was described as being "…of a very decrepit appearance." Experts later put her as suffering from senile decay.

Hannah was already caring for Annie's four and six-year-old children and agreed to take on the baby as well. It was noted by the workhouse authorities and Agnes Lewis (Annie's sister) that the baby was in good health when it left the workhouse and entered the Helen Street house.

Annie got herself some charring jobs at which she worked for many of the hours of the day, with various employers. She checked on her baby every couple of days and deposited condensed milk with her mother for the newborn's feed.

On Monday 23rd December, 1901 Annie called at Helen Street and was shocked to see the physical condition of her newest child. The baby was in discomfort and pain but her mother reassured her that everything was alright and the baby would get better. She was feeding her well. A day or so later when Annie Turvey returned to see the baby it was obvious that it was in a serious condition. She called a doctor.

Doctor Williams' surgery was in Newport Road, not far away and Annie Turvey called there to ask him to visit her seriously ill baby.

It was too late. When he arrived, the child was dead.

A post-mortem showed the child weighed four pounds. The

doctor stated the abdomen was translucent, which meant that there was no fat. It was quickly ascertained that all the poor child's internal organs were healthy but there was no trace of food. The child was malnourished and had died of starvation and its demise would have been excruciatingly painful.

The authorities got to work and Hannah Lewis was arrested and charged with feloniously killing the child. She was bailed and surrendered to her bail a few days later to attend at the Assize Court. The judge added a count of manslaughter also. She was said at the court to be 66 years of age, although her daughters thought she was in her early 70s. No-one seemed to know for sure. Court reporters at the time talked of a feeble little old woman standing in the dock.

Detective Sergeant Davey dealt with the case. Davey was very active in criminal investigations in late-Victorian and early-Edwardian times, his name being prominent. Davey appears in similar arrests in baby murder investigations so he was well versed in this type of crime. His expertise would have led to conversations between himself and legal teams reflecting his personal thoughts on the crime and the perpetrator.

One of the main talking points in the case was this: should Annie Turvey have put a tiny baby into the care of her mother? A mother who appeared incapable of looking after an infant. Annie's sister was hardly ever at Helen Street, she herself undertaking menial tasks as a charwoman. Therefore, was Annie complicit in the manslaughter of the little baby? She was not charged as such by the police. It appears that the whole case was one of an impoverished and tragic family deeply engrained in the savage lifestyle of many people of the time.

Who was the father? There seemed, as usual, no responsibility at all on the police to further that line of enquiry. Was the woman emotionally forced into sex, raped, or did she became pregnant during a period of prostitution? Or did she simply just have sex freely? We do not know.

Hannah Lewis, who was standing in the dock, was described

as lazy by staff at the workhouse. She had entered the workhouse when on bail for the charge she was currently on trial for. The staff said she would sit there and not help herself, and that she expected a mug of tea to be brought to her rather than fetch it herself, which she was capable of doing, in their opinion. There were other comments introduced into the court hearing regarding the laziness of Hannah Lewis. Evidence of Hannah's character was being promulgated as one reason for the child's death.

The defence to the charges against Hannah would obviously be that she had no intention to kill the child, either by knowingly and wilfully neglecting it. Examining what is known of the facts there may have been a stronger case of neglect against, the mother, Annie Turvey, if indeed she knew her mother was an inadequate stand-in.

At the trial, it was ascertained that Hannah Lewis was receiving only about 7/- (35p) a week to care for herself and her children. A figure astonishingly low even for 1901/2.

The trial seemed from its commencement that it was heading for only one verdict. The verdict came from the jury: 'Guilty of manslaughter', but with a strong recommendation of mercy. That recommendation was adhered to by the judge. He sentenced her to a nominal period of imprisonment, which, as Hannah had served some days in custody, meant that she was immediately released. It is not known whether she went straight back to the workhouse or to Helen Street.

What happened next to Annie's two children and in fact Annie, cannot be ascertained, but a good guess is they lived in poverty for the rest of their lives. On the other hand, we hear the tales of hard-working mothers, in great adversity, managing to bring up family members successfully who go on through the generations to achieve great things.

It seems the strict morality of Victorian times relating to unmarried mothers prevailed, and subsequently littered the lower echelons of society with injustices, hard times, and unwanted children.

ANOTHER DAY, ANOTHER CHILD

An express train between Swansea and Cardiff during the year of 1904 was scheduled to arrive at 11.15pm and was on time. A porter at the station assisted passengers arriving on the train, and saw them off the station as well as he could. There were no tickets bought for the train as Cardiff was its terminating destination. The booking office was a stone's throw from the residential terraced streets of Temperancetown.

He continued his duties until 11.40pm, at which time he saw the body of a baby placed on a locker. He called the police.

Doctors examined the baby and found no evidence of a killing, either by poisoning or violence. It was thought that the baby died of convulsions.

At the Coroner's Court, there being no evidence of death by a murderous intent, it was held that the baby died of natural causes. The police were not looking for a suspect so the investigation into the baby's death was abandoned. It would be highly unlikely the parent or parents could been traced.

The child was laid in a pauper's grave at the expense of the public purse.

* * *

The Cardiff Coroner was complaining that child murders were occurring all too frequently and surely there could be better methods employed in prevention and detection of them. He was hearing again of another baby, who'd definitely had an independent life, who was found in a brook near the railway at Canton. The baby had been sewn up in an apron before being deposited in the water.

* * *

Found in the River Taff in the mud near the town centre, on the Grangetown side, was a baby tied up in a sack. It was a few days old. Tied around its neck was a rag. It showed no signs of violent attack. It was felt it had probably died and then been 'sacked up' and thrown into the river, but landed on the mud and stayed *in situ*.

* * *

What appeared to be a three-day old baby girl was pulled out of the Glamorgan Canal near where *The Old Glendower Pub* used to be situated. The baby was naked and it was surmised it was just thrown in the water to get rid of it. One more unsolved mystery for the coroner.

* * *

The naked body of a few days' old baby was found by a road sweeper in a lane behind Corbett Road. It was impossible to identify. It would go into an unmarked, unnamed pauper's grave.

A HUSSY OR VICTIM? MARY PETERSON MAHONEY

The tragic and disturbing story of Mary Peterson Mahoney, a servant, just 18 years of age, shows once more the awful lives of many in domestic servitude. Coined 'The Whitchurch Murder', by all contemporary newspapers this case had one identical aspect to the Dingle Murder, that being the dead body of a newborn baby. The police investigation was wholly different, as was the explanation and outcome.

Ffynonwen Farm was at Whitchurch and it was here that Mary carried on her employment as a domestic servant. There are several references to Ffynnonwen farms or houses in the northern part of Cardiff. *Ffynnonwen* translated means, old spring or fountain. This was at a time when there was a distinct separation between Cardiff town (the centre as we now know it) and the suburbs we know today; Whitchurch, Pantmawr and Thornhill. These were rural areas with farmhouses surrounded by pasture. It is more than likely the Ffynnonwen farm discussed in the below case was the one standing at the bottom of today's Heol Ffynnonwen in Pantmawr.

The year is 1878. Farm servant, James Watkins, had reason to go into the store at the back of his farmhouse. He saw there, stuffed behind some sacks, a bundle tied up with what appeared to be an apron. Part of it was open and he saw what he thought was a tiny hand, a baby's hand. He realised that the only course of action he could take was to go to the local police station as fast as he could. He took the bundle to the farm granary where he locked it inside before setting off.

Watkins returned with Police Constable Hill, and he unlocked the granary and showed the officer the bundle. PC Hill opened it and found the body of a baby covered in what appeared to be coal dust. The body was dirty and black.

The officer was introduced to servant girl Mary Peterson Mahoney, who said, "It's mine. It was delivered on Friday night or Saturday morning." She was immediately arrested and conveyed to the police station and placed in detention. It was a swift outcome to a serious crime. Body found, police called, offender arrested!

In the cell, she told the officer that she went into the toilet during the early hours of the morning. There, on her own, she gave birth to a child. The baby started to make noises, whimpering and crying. Mary was petrified to think that her mistress would hear cries and she would be dismissed. She went to the coal house and got the coal pick. Mary returned to the toilet and hit the baby with all her might on the head. It would have been instantaneous death.

The surgeon acting for the coroner at the inquest said that the child was fully developed and a 'fine infant'. Externally he noticed abrasions on the left leg and that the nose and chin were wounded and scratched. There was an awful puncture wound on the forehead which had all the signs of, as Mary had said, being hit with force by a coal pick. Other damage to the forehead was consistent with being struck with the pick. The doctor was adamant that the child had an independent existence from his mother.

It was as though poor Mary, in total fear of her employers, had completely lost her mind in silencing the utterings of her baby. One can only imagine the scene in that farmhouse toilet. A tragic and frightened young girl in total distress, or was she a cold, calculating murderess?

The police took statements from all concerned and Mary was committed to the Assizes for trial on a murder charge. She was now in an unusual mental state, considering her position. She laughed a lot and cried a lot, while walking round and round her cell at Cardiff Gaol.

Reverend Father Ackroyd, a Roman Catholic Priest, attended with Mary nearly every day. He noted her mental state and tried to suppress the extreme behaviour she was exhibiting. The Reverend Father was also aware that, in all probability, Mary would be sentenced to death and he tried to prepare her for it. He gave Holy Communion daily and spent many hours at her side. It appeared that with his pastoral assistance, Mary got stronger and showed fewer signs of extreme agitation. She seemed to be getting gentle and caring help from the staff, especially the medical officer and the priest. She repeatedly admitted the killing of her baby, but it appears no-one knew who the father was. To all intents and purposes, it was not a relevant part of the case.

Surprisingly, she pleaded not guilty to murder at the Winter Assizes in Swansea. Her legal representative wondered whether her earlier admissions could be relied upon, because of her consistently poor mental condition. Perhaps this was a case where a manslaughter conviction would suffice. He said she was confused and strange in her demeanour, it was as though she was crying out for attention. Were her admissions statements of facts?

There were around twenty members of the public in court who made their presence felt in their mumblings, hateful stares, boos, and catcalling. The judge warned them to behave, which in most part they did but the damage had been done. Their antagonistic attitude got to the prisoner.

It was a long and difficult hearing and Mary's conduct in the dock caused even the most compassionate members of the jury to get upset. Mary cried, then rocked back and forth gripping the dock railings. She would stop crying, stare towards the jury, then break down again in tears. This diminutive young lady was in a state of extreme distress.

To repeat something that has been said before. Whilst researching this trial there is one piece of the jigsaw that it is missing. Who was the father of the baby? We simply do not know what emotional or physical force was used on the girl, but what we do know is that the man got away with it and the girl did not. She was the 'loose woman', the 'hussy' and there to be judged. It was not the man who had killed the baby but surely there was a modicum of responsibility on him?

An investigating police officer in the modern era would ask the obvious question: "Who was the father and did he force you to have sex?"

Anyone who has served on a jury will know that there is a mixture of emotions when coming to a decision. The facts as told to the court may be compelling and there may appear to be only one finding, but human emotions can come into play. It would appear that in Mary's case 'disgust' may have been the overriding reason for finding the young servant girl guilty. After all, however sorry one may feel for an individual, however great is the desire for retribution, the jury members must bring in a verdict based on the evidence as presented. Jury members were well aware that finding Mary guilty of murder, in essence, meant sentencing her to death themselves.

They found her 'guilty', there would have been no other verdict, but the foreman then continued: "We would make a strong recommendation for mercy."

Mary was asked by the clerk to the court whether she had something to say with regard to the probable ultimate sentence that was to come to her. Mary was standing in the dock gripping the bannister tightly. She seemed speechless, in a state of shock. She tried to speak but nothing came out of her mouth.

The judge donned the black cap and spoke.

> *"Mary Peterson Mahoney, the jury, in common with every person in the Court, must deeply feel compassionate for your situation, but they have felt compelled by their duty to their country to find you guilty of the crime of the murder of an infant child, of which you*

had been delivered. I will not endeavour to harrow up your feelings, which, if you are at all sensible of the awful position in which you are placed by your conduct, it will be quite unnecessary for me to do. The jury have accompanied their verdict by a strong recommendation to mercy, but I hold out no hope whatever for my part, because I have no authority to do so. I have only to pass the sentence of the law, but I will take care that the recommendation which the jury made is transmitted to the Secretary of State for the Home Department, who, in the exercise of his duty, will say whether the circumstances will enable him to spare your life. I have no power to do so, and can only pass upon you the dread sentence of the law, which is that you be taken to the place from whence you came, and thence to the place of execution, and there hanged by the neck until you are dead, and that your body be afterwards carried to the precincts of the prison in which you were last confined after conviction. And may the Lord have mercy on your soul."

Mary started to shake, then screamed, and went berserk. She fought with the guards, completely out of control, and it was with difficulty that she was taken down into the bowels of the courtroom and thrown screeching into a cell.

Mary was taken by train from Swansea to Cardiff, her escort included the Governor of the County Gaol. When she arrived at Cardiff Gaol, a Roman Catholic chaplain, Reverend Father Ackroyd, was immediately in attendance. Mary had stopped eating and was refusing food, the enormity of the sentence seemed to have hit home leaving her distraught. The teenager's mental condition had plummeted and she was giving cause for concern to all around her. The medical officers noted that she was often delirious to the point of insanity. Her conversational abilities reduced to incoherent and mindless rambling.

Behind the scenes there was frantic activity from a variety of sources. It seemed everyone involved in the case, the judge, the High Sheriff, the Roman Catholic Church, the Cardiff Prison Governor, and women's rights societies were pleading for respite from the ultimate sentence. The judge's comments at the conclusion of the case, together with a plea for mercy from the jury, and a strong public petition, came to the notice of the Home Secretary – the only person with the power to commute a death sentence.

One week later a communication was sent from London to the High Sheriff of Glamorgan.

> *Sir, I am to signify to you the Queen's commands that the execution of the sentence of death passed on Mary Peterson Mahoney, now in the Cardiff prison, be respited until further signification of Her Majesty's pleasure. I am Sir, your obedient servant.*

The news was conveyed to Mary by the prison governor but it appears she found it difficult to comprehend. The staff tried to calm her and explain but it would appear she did not understand why she was going back to Swansea Assize Court. At the court her sentence was reduced by the judge from the death sentence to 15 years' penal servitude, a sentence which was very severe but not, of course, terminal. Mary was returned to Cardiff Gaol to commence her sentence.

The Reverend Father visited her and commented that she was once again agitated and deeply upset. She was dancing and singing, some said she was like a maniac. It was at this time that they found out that Mary had severe epileptic fits as a youngster.

Christian groups and others still could not bear the thought that Mary would be sent to serve prison life and undertake hard labour. Her predicament appears to have been followed very closely by many women's groups of the era.

The idea of a young girl giving birth on her own, then being so scared she would be found out and savagely murdering her newborn, was repulsive to women's and Christian groups. Young girls in servitude were often being used by employers and men in general for their own pleasures, the girls being to scared to say no. Others though thought that she must pay for her crime and do the fifteen years.

When Father Ackroyd saw Mary again in prison after the good news, he noted that she was 'not in a good place'. Often, she would lie on the floor or appear to have convulsions. Mary told him that she was unaware of what happened at the Whitchurch farm but she knew that she had done something 'naughty'.

Mary signed letters of thanks to all the people who had assisted in her plea for leniency, even though she did not remember what she had done wrong. Her basic courtesy and manners did not go unnoticed by those around her.

On the 7th July, 1884, several years into her sentence, the East Glamorgan Prisoner's Aid Society arranged for Mary to leave and be admitted to a care home where she could be looked after.

Mary's sad life, the tragic demise of her baby, the subsequent trials, and the sentence of death blew the teenager's life away. The event of infanticide must surely carry with it overwhelming guilt. Her life was virtually over as soon as she entered into the act of sexual intercourse that resulted in her pregnancy. The savage world of Victorian standards, morals, and protocol put Mary in the Assize Court dock.

Surely the only reason for the demise of the baby was the fear of losing a job, income, and respect. Societal values were that harsh. It is to be wondered whether Mary was forced into intercourse, which is likely, and what happened to the man? Who was he? Did anyone try to find out? Probably not. In the words of one of the reports of the time, it was the "…loose moralled hussy" who brought it on herself.

Ffynnonwen Farm still exists and is located at Pantmawr Road and its junction with Caer Wenallt. In the 1870s it was the centre of a large farm complex but today it is part of the housing estate in Pantmawr Road and directly in front is Whitchurch Golf Club. In late Victorian times there was a distinct separation between Cardiff town (the centre as we now know it), and the outlying areas of Whitchurch, Rhiwbina, and Pantmawr. These were rural areas with farmhouses surrounded by outhouses, barns, and pasture.

CHAPTER TEN

Harry Houdini in Cardiff Magistrates Court

The Empire Theatre, Cardiff

Hungarian, Erich Weisz, moved with his parents to the United States of America in 1874. By the time of his death in 1926, his stage name of Harry Houdini, was recognised the world over. It was then, as it is today, a name that is synonymous with extreme escapology.

One of the most illustrious theatre buildings in Cardiff is now, and has been for many years, a *J.D. Wetherspoons* public house. Its main entrance is in Westgate Street, virtually opposite the Principality Stadium but the entrance at the rear of the building in Womanby Street will perhaps hold more memories. It was the stage door.

It was in 1904 that the Grand Theatre of Varieties was renamed the Kings Theatre. It lasted only a few years before the name was changed again to the Palace Theatre. No doubt the biggest star to appear at the theatre in its short life as the Kings was none other than Harry Houdini.

Houdini was world famous, his daring and seemingly impossible illusions and escapology displays were well known but not so well known was when Harry got himself into trouble in Cardiff.

Houdini had appeared all over South Wales playing to packed houses in Newport, Cardiff, and Swansea. On one visit to Cardiff though he fell foul of the law and with it showed that the great man had a weakness: insecurity, or perhaps arrogance. He thought himself the best escapologist in the world, especially when it came to handcuffs. His main music-hall act was stunning audiences with his skill at escaping, even inviting some theatre-goers to give it a try, always resulting in failure.

On his arrival in Cardiff one evening, Houdini heard some amazing news. There was another handcuff escape artist in town. While he was appearing at the Kings Theatre another artist, Hilbert, was entertaining the crowds at the nearby Empire Theatre miraculously escaping from handcuffs.

To further the annoyance of Houdini the local media were

referring to both performers as the best handcuff escapees in the country, using the tag, 'The Handcuff King'. Houdini heard that his rival was going to give away the secrets of the great escapes. Houdini was livid.

What went through his mind, apart from jealousy and rage, was how to counteract and get rid of his counterpart. Houdini was the 'Handcuff King', he knew it and the world knew it. What was to be done? He conceived a plan.

It is said he obtained a false moustache from the theatre props room and pressed it into place on his top lip. He also took some talcum powder and whitened his hair, and borrowed a walking stick. He was happy that he was now unrecognisable as a global superstar. He was on a mission.

It is alleged that a few minutes into Hilbert's performance Harry Houdini stood up, waving a pair of his handcuffs and shouted, "Fraud! You're a fraud. I've got a pair of handcuffs here you couldn't get off!'

The disturbance led to the Empire Theatre manager ordering his staff to forcibly remove the troublemaker. Struggling, Houdini was dragged along the aisle and to the side exit by theatre staff and then into the hands of police constables.

The theatregoers witnessed the curious event, some standing to get a better view of the altercation. They were certainly getting their money's worth that evening. One wonders what the performer on the stage was thinking though. The staff pushed open an exit door and unceremoniously dumped Houdini into the adjacent alleyway. In the fracas Houdini injured his leg. He hailed a cab to take him back to the Kings Theatre in Westgate Street.

The whole affair ended up in the Cardiff Police Courts when Houdini took out a summons against the theatre manager, Mr Lea, for assault and gave his version of events. Houdini told the magistrates that he was not happy when he heard that Hilbert was going to expose his secrets. He went to the Empire and sat in the six-penny seats for the 7.00pm performance. He only spoke once to say, "I have a pair of handcuffs here you could not open."

"That's all I said," he said before he was grabbed by many men and the police.

Houdini then claimed he had heard a police constable say to the theatre manager, Mr Lea, "What shall I do Mr Lea?"

Lea shouted out "Throw him out!"

He said he saw Lea running across the aisle and jumped at him and he had said, 'I will show you!' he then maintained that Lea grabbed him by the throat with both hands and was tearing at his collar. Houdini told the court: "He put his leg between mine and said 'We've been waiting for you.'"

He said then he was thrown against a constable, striking his knee against one of the seats as he fell. He thought the constable "...had done me." There was laughter after Mr Lea replied to a question put to him by the magistrate: "Why did it take four theatre staff, three constables and yourself to tackle one man and eject him?" Lea replied, "He's a professional gaol-breaker, Sir." (Referring to his famous trick of escaping from police cells).

The magistrate asked Mr Lea if he assaulted Houdini. He replied, "If I had, perhaps he would have suffered more."

The magistrate dismissed the summons much to the chagrin of Houdini. Back in the King's Theatre on 11th April, 1905 Houdini topped the bill and he noted that the place was packed, every seat being sold out. 'The Handcuff King and the Gaol Breaker' did all his tricks, bar one. His damaged leg prevented that.

Sensationally, the matter did not end there. Houdini stayed in the area appearing at the Newport Lyceum. It was on 20th April, 1905 that the Chief Constable gave Houdini and Hilbert permission to use one of his cells and handcuffs to demonstrate who was the best escapologist in the world. Hilbert had intimated it would be the real test of who was the greatest.

It was at 4.00pm that Houdini presented himself at the police station cells to the Chief Constable. He was told to wait as Hilbert had not yet arrived. By now a massive crowd had gathered and was growing all the time. It was taking a huge effort from the constables guarding their station to keep the crowd out.

Hilbert had still not turned up so Houdini, with several press men following, entered the police cells and was shown to cell number nine. He undressed himself totally and his clothes were taken into the custody of a senior police officer. The cell was searched and sealed with Houdini within. Each cell door in the old police stations had a small, lockable hatch that could be slammed shut, this Houdini wanted left open. It was just big enough to push a plate through. Cell doors are only lockable from the outside and the senior officer had possession of the master key.

The police and the media then walked to the end of the cell block, as requested by Houdini and then they were out of sight.

Five minutes later Houdini, now dressed, walked up the cell block corridor towards the assembled spectators. He had also managed to open the adjoining cell to get his clothes, with no key, and then opened another gate that sealed the cell block. There was a palpable feeling of shock among the onlookers.

News filtered out to the thousands outside and when he appeared he was cheered and followed by the crowd all the way to the stage door of the Lyceum. Houdini had guaranteed a sell out at his show that week.

One wonders if one of the Cardiff constables obtained Houdini's autograph in exchange for a favour. It is doubtful, but the Newport officers may have been a little more successful. Records aren't clear as to what happened to Hilbert.

CHAPTER ELEVEN

Cardiff's wildest publican

The Glamorgan Canal at Mill Lane, on the right the houses of New Street, adjacent to Charlotte Street, where the Flying Eagle was located.

As a young police officer, I knew many pub landlords. I visited *The Loudoun, The Salutation, The Bomb And Dagger, The Blue Anchor, The Freemasons, The Torbay, The Fishguard, The Quebec, The Cornish Mount, The Greyhound, The George, The Bute Road*

Tavern, The Rothesay Castle, The Machen Forge, and *The Lord Wimborne,* to name but a few former Cardiff pubs. Each pub had very different landlords or landladies, each a character in their own right and each kept discipline in their own way. They had a similar job to a police officer, only on a smaller scale: law and order, and staying within the rules, in charge and constantly having to be aware of everyone within their establishment. Every publican knew their locals and knew when strangers were in. It was a different breed of publican in those days, as it was a different style of policing.

I held publicans in great esteem. It seemed they were all-powerful and everyone wanted to be their friend. The majority were exceptional at their job. They had their own unique way of ejecting drunken customers. One used to put the music on the juke box so loud that everyone was screaming at her to switch it off, but she would not until the drunk was unceremoniously bundled out by the music or fellow customers.

One back street pub near Bute Street Police Station used to send one of the 'girls' around to the nick to get some help in throwing someone out. It always worked. Officers knew that the reward was a swift half in the back room later that evening. One publican was so drunk by early evening he could be found slumped on the bar until his barmaids shut the pub and slammed the door. They left him there. First thing in the morning he was up and about to be seen wandering down to the newsagents to get his papers, with not a care in the world. He would go back and clean up his premises in readiness for opening up again that night.

He was a real character, but one name stands out more than all the rest – Mad Jack Matthews. No other person grabbed the headlines in Victorian Cardiff more than Mad Jack! His violent and criminal exploits lit up the courts and the newspapers for nearly half a century. His death on 3rd July, 1888 in London saw the end of an era.

It was during his time as landlord in residence of *The Flying Eagle* public house in Charlotte Street that his notoriety was born.

The street passed roughly west / east across where the *Marriott Hotel* is now situated. It was a constant source of violence and altercation. Luckily for some, but unluckily for others, the street was demolished around 1875/6 and with it Mad Jack's pub.

Jack was born in Northern Ireland around 1823 to reputable parents who put him to work as an apprentice to a trader in Belfast, but this did not last long. His temper was causing him problems that led to a situation which saw many of his colleagues refusing to work alongside him, let alone attempt to manage him.

As many parents did at that time, they enrolled their son into the army. He joined the 14th Foot and was sent to England. The discipline in regiments in those days was seen as an important part of a young man's development. In Jack's case, it wasn't. His constant rebelliousness and insubordination led to frequent floggings and imprisonment.

Unfortunately, no punishment could calm down the rebel in him and his bouts of temper grew ever more intense as the treatment he received worsened. On numerous occasions he had to be restrained by several army guards. This was at a time when soldiers were subject to intense discipline and sometimes barbaric regimes in an attempt to prepare them for frontline battle.

The army finally sacked Jack and classified him as 'incorrigible'. This, in effect, said that Jack was permanently incapable of improvement or reform and was destined to always be unemployable and be a nuisance. He moved to Sheffield where his job as a cutler (a seller of knives, forks, and spoons) lasted only a few months. He found there was money to be earned by sharpening knives and razors on the streets. He bought a small handcart and sharpening wheel and carried on this trade for some time. With a temper like Jack's the last thing one would have thought would be good for him was to be in possession of cut-throat razors.

How he ended up in Cardiff is not known, but he did, and so did his cart and wheel. He worked the Newtown and Central streets sharpening scissors and razors. It must have brought him in a little money, as he soon became proprietor of a small ale-house at 21, Adam Street at the age of 38 years. He was married to Ellen and had a daughter named Jane, in 1861. Jack was getting around his 'patch' and squaring up to anyone he took a dislike to.

Few Victorian photographs survive of Adam Street, and this grainy shot shows the street where Jack acquired an ale house.

In 1863 Jack got involved with a woman in Louisa Street, Butetown. Their arguing soon turned to fisticuffs and the police were called. Two officers attended and Jack turned his attention on to them. His temper reached boiling point and he was taken, fighting and screaming, to the police station. He was charged with assaulting the police officers and fined £2.10.0d for each offence. This was heard at the Cardiff Police court on 7th November, 1862. To put the fine of £2.10.0d into context, when Charlotte Street was constructed the ground rent for a year on number 32 was £2.10.0d. (£2.50p) Incidentally, next door at number 31 was later to become one of the most notorious houses in the street with the police calling time and time again to arrest persons within for prostitution, brothel keeping, robbery, and wounding.

Jack's ill-gotten gains elevated him to lodging house owner. Cardiff Docks was growing and the industrious neighbourhoods surrounding the shipping wharfs brought in thousands of sailors every year, all looking for a good time. Someone had to service their needs.

One thing was for sure, the Charlotte Street area was notorious. Dance halls, brothels, drinking dens, and disorderly houses, were the norm and Jack was doing well out of them.

There were other licensed pubs in Charlotte Street such as *The Sailor's Return, Albion, Irish Harp, Ship, Jolly Sailor, Cornish Arms, Kings Arms Brew House* and the oddly named *Lame Chicken*. Add to those a host of unlicensed beer houses, and this one short street must have been a hive of activity, and was an area known for robberies and violence.

Sailors lodged in Jack's houses and drank in his pub. He acquired slum lodging houses in Whitmore Lane, virtually adjacent to Charlotte Street

As early as the 1840s the area of Whitmore Lane, China Row and Charlotte Street was notorious for its awful conditions and its seedy inhabitants. Annie Anthony was just a teenager in 1847 when she was beaten, as was numerous other local girls, by a man named John Thomas. It was the legendary Superintendent Stockdale, (the first chief of police in Cardiff), who told local magistrates: "He is a desperate fellow, he kicks and knocks about the girls as a boy would a football. He beats them periodically."

It was a front-room pub that Annie and her friend were beaten in by Thomas, he even threw his pint glass at them. Both were injured. It was common practice in the Charlotte Street area for men to follow women who had earned some cash doing 'business', and then rob them, beating them up in the process. A local vicar called Reverend Thomas, in court branded Jack 'depraved' and with all that evidence piled up against him the magistrate sentenced him to a fine of £5, a massive amount, and if non-payment followed he was to spend two months in prison. He left the court a free man.

The area was described as 'vile' and warranted constant police attention, and one public house was at the centre of their scrutiny, *The Flying Eagle*. Just a hundred yards or so from the pub was one of Cardiff's worst streets, Mary Ann Street, home to many more public houses, now long-forgotten: *The Operative Tavern, The Nicholls Arms, The Butchers Arms, The Parrot Tavern, The Cork and Waterford* to name a few.

The Flying Eagle was growing in reputation especially in regard to the disposal of stolen property acquired via street robberies and thefts. Many a sailor told the tale of being robbed by one or more prostitutes and then chasing their assailants towards this pub where they would run inside. Unfortunately, when the sailors attempted to enter the same the door it was slammed shut and bolted from inside. Mad Jack Matthews was akin to Charles Dickens' Fagin and running a very profitable business, not with youngsters pickpocketing on the streets, but with women stealing from clients and disposing of their gains through him.

The police were in constant touch with Jack and it was noted at the time that he hated the police with some venom. This brought him to Court on many occasions for fighting or receiving stolen property. There seemed no way that police officers could arrest Jack for robbery, he left that for others to perform, his function was to receive their ill-gotten gains.

The police had their hands full and Jack was not the only pub licensee to be causing problems. A massive sum of money, £33, was stolen from an Irish cattle dealer when he was taken to a brothel at the end of Charlotte Street near Bute Street. The owner of the brothel, Mrs King of *The Ship Inn*, Bute Street was arrested. The case came to nothing as the cattle dealer returned to Ireland and so she was released.

Jack Matthews had a weakness, and that was gold watches. Rumour had it that his stash of them that would have enabled him to purchase a palace. He was often seen in court showing off his new watches to all and sundry, which infuriated both police and judiciary alike.

The Golden Cross 2017. Charlotte Street ran behind where the Marriott now stands.

It was noted though that he was generous to others, conjuring up images of a Robin Hood type character. Perhaps there was method in Jack's madness in this. If a man had been in prison he could approach Jack, who would put him up in one of his lodging houses and give him money. In this he portrayed a charitable disposition to some, but to others his charity was a ruse to gain more stolen property and money. Jack was now a rich man in relative terms to the other local inhabitants. He had found a route out of poverty.

Jack Matthews hated the police, indeed any type of authority. That hatred was to manifest itself on numerous occasions. There were times when he won his battles with law and order.

The year was 1863. The infamous Mad Jack Matthews is, once again, causing trouble in West Bute Street. One police constable attempts to arrest him and in doing so has to "...hit him hard." Another constable tried to stop his colleague from striking Matthews. Mad Jack then stood between the two policemen like a referee in a prize fight. The result was that *both* policemen were suspended from duty. Mad Jack had a charge of assaulting a police officer dismissed in court. The first officer was warned about his future conduct. The second was sacked on the grounds of 'Lacking in moral courage'.

MAD JACK'S ARREST SHEET

Jack's court appearances were too numerous to list in full. Here is a selection:

1862. Assaulting the police in Louisa Street. He had lost his temper and was said at the time to be only wearing a Guernsey smock (this woollen gown that reached to the knee dates from the Middle Ages). Fined £2.

1862. Summoned for keeping a brothel and ordered to close it immediately. Failed to do so. Sent to prison for one month.

1863. Refused to let police enter *The Flying Eagle* pub to investigate robbery. Fined £1.

1863. Illegally opened *The Flying Eagle*. Fined 5/-.

1864. Arrested in *Fishguard Arms*, Bute Street. Offence: "...being drunk and riotous in Bute Street." Fined 5/-.

1864 Arrested in *Flying Eagle* for being drunk and causing a disturbance which required three policeman to restrain him. Eliza Davies, who lived with him, accused policeman of striking her. Dismissed due to uncertain evidence.

1864. Threatening language to Charlotte Grey of

Pembrokeshire Arms, Charlotte Street causing her bodily fear and to faint with shock. Witnesses testified Grey had provoked him by calling him a thief. Bound over for 3 months. Grey cautioned and charged costs. Witness was Robert Dolbear of the *Six Bells Inn*.

1864. Matthews and Elizabeth Davies accused of assaulting a woman. Case dismissed due to conflicting evidence. Also charged with indecent exposure in *Flying Eagle*. Case dismissed due to unreliable evidence.

1864. Charged with selling beer during prohibited hours and assaulting the policeman investigating the offence. Matthews claimed customers were gathering early on Sunday morning to go to Llandaff Fair and needed refreshments. Fined £2 plus costs.

1864. Matthews involved in quarrel with a woman in *Flying Eagle* who bought beer there to sell on to others. She claimed he struck her causing injuries, which he denied. Found guilty and sentenced to one month's hard labour.

1864. On release from prison Mathews accused two neighbours of removing items from *Flying Eagle* without his permission. Case adjourned for further enquiries and later dismissed for lack of evidence.

1864. Charged with keeping an improper house and assaulting a policeman investigating the offence. He objected to their conduct in searching the pub and so Jack used force to stop them. Charge incorrectly entered in official book. Ordered to keep the peace for six months on two bonds of £40 each.

1864. As a result of the above case, Matthews wrote a letter of complaint to the council's Watch Committee claiming police intimidation. He claimed *Flying Eagle* and similar places were safety valves of society that should be protected. His letter was reported to have caused the Watch Committee some amusement. After questioning Superintendent Stockdale on "…unnecessary interference by police in Charlotte Street area," no further action was taken.

1864. During the trial of two people charged with robbery Matthews was blamed for aiding their escape by shutting the doors to prevent pursuit by police when they fled through *The Flying Eagle*. Fined £3 plus costs for refusing to admit entry to the police.

1864. Constable Evans was brought before the court on a private summons of assaulting the landlord, John Yarwood, of the *Excavator Arms* in Charlotte Street. The officer denied the charge vigorously, and the allegation that he threatened to get Matthews and Yarwood deported to Australia. PC Evans alleged that Mad Jack had paid cash to Yarwood and his solicitor in an effort to get PC Evans convicted and sacked. The case was dismissed against the officer.

1865. Appeared in court blood-stained and with head injuries. Charged with assaulting PC Evans when he was investigating whether 17, Whitmore Lane, adjoining rear of *Flying Eagle*, was a brothel. When Matthews saw Evans he became violent and attacked him, then followed him after he left and repeated the assault outside Pollards grocery store, 264, Bute Street. Matthews tried to run away but was restrained with difficulty and taken into custody by Evans and two other constables. Matthews complained of entrapment and provocation by police officers who wanted the authorities to deport him. The deportation of criminals was to cease in 1868. He also denied owning 17, Whitmore Lane. On account of his injuries the fine was reduced to £2 plus costs. There were other cases of women using 17 Whitmore Lane for prostitution in which Matthews was involved.

1865 Charged with assaulting PC Evans whilst he was pursuing suspected thieves in Charlotte Street. Jack challenged Evans repeatedly using bad language and tried to warn other occupants in the street of the police presence. Bound over for twelve months to keep the peace at £50 plus two sureties of £25. Two very brave, (or optimistic if they thought Jack wouldn't re-offend), men came forward: Mr Higgins of 31, Charlotte Street and Mr Bennett of Mary Ann Street. They paid the sureties into the court. Jack was then in trouble straight away as he caught sight of two journalists from the *Cambrian Daily Leader*. He threatened them and started tearing down newspaper notices that he alleged were bringing his good name into public contempt. He was again warned about his conduct and bound over to keep the peace for 12 months for £50. Amazingly, the two previous sureties were not forfeited.

1865 Arrested for assaulting two women in *Flying Eagle*. Jack claimed one woman hit him with a bottle when they were fighting with a third woman. The women appeared in court with black eyes. Jack was fined £1.

1865 Police officer passing *The Flying Eagle* heard cries of murder coming from inside. He went in to investigate and saw Jack in a fierce fight with a woman who "…sometimes passed as his wife." When the officer tried to restrain Jack, the woman turned on him. A violent altercation followed with three more police officers arriving. It took the four of them to get Jack to a police station, fighting all the way. The defence witness stated that the police had "…staffed' him and hit him with their torches." Found guilty and fined £2.

MAD JACK MATTHEWS STANDS FOR THE COUNCIL

In October, 1865 Mad Jack Matthews had enough of the authorities. He applied a motto to himself, well-earned he thought, of 'Morality, Intelligence and Co-operation'. He decided to stand for the Cardiff Borough Council. He had printed a leaflet headed, *To the free and independent electors of the south ward* and started to put about his election campaign.

He accused the town councillors of 'snoring and snoozing' when they should have been attending to their moral duties. He promised to oppose "…humbug, pride, jobbery, favouritism, peculation and unnecessary expense." He criticised the police, accusing them of victimising innocent people. One wonders if it was PC Evans he had in mind.

He had a go at the local newspapers who had questioned how he had got away with so much. A recurring headline about Jack in newspapers was him being treated with "…the utmost leniency and forbearance."

Another grainy photograph from 1878. A rare view of St Mary Street Police Station (the building to the right of picture) – Mad Jack's second home.

He hired committee rooms in *The Bath Arms* in St Mary Street for his followers to meet and plan a strategy. This pub was conveniently next to the town hall and police station.

The election was on 3rd November, 1865 and there were seven candidates on the list. During the day, Jack raced around the south ward of the central part of town knocking on doors and lobbying people to get out and vote for him. He calculated that he was in the lead with all and sundry promising their vote. Unfortunately for

Jack out of the seven names on the list he was seventh! He polled just 15 votes. However, it did not end there. He was sued for the £1 he owed for hiring the committee room. It went on for a long time but at the culmination in County Court he was ordered to pay £1, plus costs.

The Bath Arms *(left in the photograph), where Jack held his election meetings.*

Jack Matthews was quoted as saying:

> *"I don't think there's a man breathing that is so imposed upon as I've been in this town, or a man treated worse."*

In December, 1865 two police officers tried to enter his pub, and he attacked them. Numerous people joined in, but he was arrested and appeared in court. Most of the witnesses contradicted each other and it was a mess. He was fined £5 with a warning: next time he would go to prison.

There were many people who were sick to death of how Matthews was continuously avoiding prison, avoiding being held to account when bound over to keep the peace, and avoiding having his sureties followed up properly. This came to the notice of the Editor of the *Cardiff Times*. In March, 1866 there appeared an editorial in the newspaper attacking the lenient handling of Mad Jack Matthew. It was headed, *The Dangerous Classes and the Local Authorities*. It asked how he had managed to thwart proceedings against him and posed the question: 'How does he get away with it?' It was a direct challenge to the Watch Committee.

The Cardiff Watch Committee met monthly and for several months thereafter, Matthews was on the agenda. They did not like criticism. There was a problem though and the problem was serious, they all disagreed on how to go ahead and deal with Mad Jack. Some thought the legal costs would be too expensive, others that "...the biggest ruffian in Cardiff should not be allowed to break his bond and cheat the law." There were some councillors who thought magistrates had a soft spot for Matthews, or the 'Cardiff Pet' as he was called by one. Others thought that people were scared of him for fear of personal retribution, but all agreed *something* had to be done.

A plan of action was taken via the local magistrate courts which finally ended up at the Quarter Sessions in July of 1866. The councillors put a case against the magistrates and Jack in an attempt to force the court to recover the bail money he had often got away with not paying and to legally enforce payment. This case went to the Queen's Bench of the High Court in London. All this had taken a year and, having no end result in sight, the Cardiff Council decided to drop the case totally.

So, what was Mad Jack Matthews up to whilst all this was going on? He was continuing his furious lifestyle.

In July, accused of assaulting a woman, case dismissed, lack of evidence.

In August fined £3 for opening *Flying Eagle* pub at 8.30am, out of hours. Fined £3.

In August charged with assaulting a boarding house keeper who owed him money. Case dismissed.

In August charged with brutal assault on a woman living at *Flying Eagle*. The most pleasing of outcomes for many people: he was sent to prison for one month's hard labour.

In November 1866 he was charged with threatening police officers who were preventing him from violently assaulting a woman. Case dismissed as the police had undertaken the wrong procedures.

And it went on. It was known that Matthews went to ground for some time, and travelled around the country. When he came back it started all over again.

In June 1868, Matthews suffered a cut mouth during a fight with a man armed with a knife. The man was fined £2 plus costs.

In September 1868, Matthews and others accused of causing a disturbance in Caroline Street, fined 1 shilling.

In February 1869, fined 5 shillings plus cost for using abusive language towards police inspector and constable.

In March 1869, charged with threatening a shop keeper and inciting others to violence. Case dismissed due to provocation.

In May 1869, fined 10 shillings plus costs for fighting and causing an obstruction in St Mary Street.

In May 1869 charged with causing injuries to a woman living with him which led to her going into the poor law union workhouse where she was found to have broken arm and ribs, and internal bleeding. Sentenced to one month hard labour.

In September 1869, under a new Act for licensing beer houses there were 59 applications including *The Flying Eagle*, that were refused.

In October 1869, accused of causing a large obstruction in Charlotte Street by offering to give away beer to a crowd. After refusing to move and protesting, the magistrates stopped him from distributing it and Matthews took the barrel back in doors. Case dismissed. An appeal for a licence to sell beer not to be drunk on the premises was refused.

In the same month, Matthew's stood for election in the South Ward reissuing his election address of 1865 with the added promise "...to prevent the streets being paved with granite for the benefit of town council men." He was again bottom of the poll with 54 votes which were said to have come from "Whitmore and Charlotte Street's roughs."

More court appearances followed but Jack still tried to get a licence to sell beer. He was repeatedly refused so he decided to sell his beer in barrels for others to sell for him. That got him into more trouble. Some people did not pay him and there were reports of serious altercations in the area.

In January 1870 he was bound over to keep the peace to the sum of £20 over threats to a woman over a non-payment of beer money. The woman, next month, accused him of assaulting her over a debt. He got off that one having the case dismissed in court.

The newspapers were in uproar attempting to find how Mad Jack Matthews always seemed to avoid justice, especially in regard to the non-application of sureties and binding over orders.

Jack then disappeared from public life with no reported appearances in court or newspapers. One would suspect that even though the media seemed to hate Jack they missed him and the extra news sheets or papers they would sell telling of his exploits.

A year later in February, 1871 Matthews was again on the daily list when charged with selling beer without a licence. Lo and behold the case was dismissed because of contradictory evidence!

The problem for the authorities was that Jack had built up a reputation and sailors came off the ships and headed straight for *The Flying Eagle*. Finding it closed they either forced their way in or were allowed admittance only to be told he had no beer. This happened one day in February, 1871 when he got into a furious fight with seamen who were demanding to be served. He was stabbed in the thigh and probably for once in his life he was *glad* to see constables arrive. Jack and the sailors went to court, with one seaman charged with wounding Jack. He was found not guilty.

Jack continued to cause disturbances in the area but it was not until July of 1872 that he was appearing in court again. He was accused of threatening a police officer with a sword but he pleaded self-defence. He said the officer was armed and he was frightened so had to defend himself. He was found guilty and once again bound over to keep the peace for a year on a surety of £50. In August, one month after his last appearance, he was fined just £2 for drunken and riotous behaviour and assaulting a police constable.

Why it was that time and time again he got off his bindings over is unfathomable today. Only his contemporaries will ever know. Examining the usual sentencing practises of the time, it is obvious that something out of the ordinary was occurring when Jack appeared in front of magistrates.

It was noted by many ex-Cardiff City Police officers from the 1960s that some persistent offenders, especially those involving drunkenness, would be treated leniently. Whether it was the 'Oh not you again' syndrome, or 'What's the point?' attitude, it is without doubt that numerous times he got off open and shut cases, dodged the punishments doled out, or received punishments that did not match the crimes.

He was a persistent abuser of women. Could it be that the women who appeared in court giving evidence were seen by the upper class bench as ne'er-do-wells themselves therefore not worthy of credence or respect? Could Jack have had some dubious links with certain members of the bench.

He must have been a charismatic man, as well as a very scary one, could that have helped? Or maybe it came down to basic human instinct of survival? Jack's uncontrollable fits of rage were well documented and the last person a magistrate would want to see whilst walking his good lady in Queen Street was Mad Jack Matthews. To be recognised as a the 'beak' who sent him down may send the man into an uncontrollable rage. Whatever we may guess, no-one will ever know the real truth.

One bit of good news for Matthews was that he was awarded one and a half guineas as costs for having to attend an Electoral

Revision Court when a Liberal party agent challenged Jack's right to vote, let alone stand for election.

The case of August 1873 did not assist the area's reputation but it did once again show Jack's amazing feats of getting away with his crimes. 16, Whitmore Lane was one of Jack's houses that was alleged as being used as a brothel and for illegal beer selling. After reports of trouble, four police constables entered the house only to be met by Jack in possession of a sword and a pistol. He was disarmed in a battle royal and put before the court. He claimed the police had acted illegally by entering the house without a warrant. The magistrates agreed, and the case was dismissed. To make matters worse one constable was fined £2 for causing Jack injuries.

The council were weary of the constant problems caused by residents of the Charlotte Street and Whitmore Lane area. They could see no answer to the problems other than to evict and demolish. Jack owned several houses and was obtaining money from rent, the illegal selling of beer on the premises, prostitution, and receiving and re-selling stolen property. Many of his women living in his houses were convicted of selling beer illegally, some were sent to prison, one thing that didn't happen too often to the 'Godfather' of Charlotte Street.

Mad Jack Matthews continued to appear in Court charged with assaulting women and police officers but all was to change and Jack disappeared.

The Conservative Home Secretary in the 1870s brought in an Act of Parliament (which many Conservatives were against) that was to assist the Cardiff Town Council in eradicating what they saw as Mad Jack's fiefdom.

The Artisans' and Labourers' Dwelling Improvement Act of 1875 was heaven sent as it allowed councils the right of compulsory purchase of slum dwellings, and then the ability to demolish them.

One can imagine the trouble when Jack heard about this, but imagine his smile when he realised that his old enemy, the town council, were going to buy houses off him for a fair price! It was not long before the Act was used to demolish Charlotte Street and much of Whitmore Lane.

With the demolition went *The Flying Eagle*, reduced to a pile of rubble in a street that was to be no more. But, of course, only a few hundred yards away was the notorious Mary Ann Street. which was not demolished under the Act. I discuss this infamous road in another book, *The Cruel Streets Revisited*. This points to the council using the Act for the specific purpose of demolishing Charlotte Street for one reason: Mad Jack Matthews.

Jack moved to 87, Severn Road, Canton, bought from the money given to him for the purchase of his properties. It was galling to say the least for some as virtually all the money used to purchase his houses was as a result of illicit activities.

It was noted that toward the end of his life he still suffered from the most outrageous bursts of temper, although his rages had lost their physical power and he was more easily controllable. It seemed after the outbursts that he apologised for what he had said and done.

It was reported that he turned to the Bible and the last days of his life were taken up by being read tracts at his bedside by a friend. The friend, a publican, witnessed Mad Jack Matthews abstain totally from alcohol and undertake Christian fellowship. Not many people believed it. The madman of *The Flying Eagle* finding religion was improbable and ridiculous, yet there is good evidence to suggest that he did.

Mad Jack moved to London and ended his days in Rendlesham Road, Clapton, Essex where he died on the 3rd July, 1888. There were more shocks to come for the good people of Cardiff.

On 16th and 17th July, 1888 Jack's belongings went on auction arranged by R. Wiltshire at *The Bluebell Hotel*, High Street. His house and furniture at Severn Road was auctioned on the 17th but it was the auction of his property the day before that set the whole town talking. It was an Aladdin's cave of jewellery including scores of gold watches, gold rings, necklaces, and other valuable items. There were revolvers, pistols, and an immense number of items collected over the decades.

In fact, in today's money the value of Jack Matthews estate would be worth a cool £250,000. There were letters sent to the local press with uncomplimentary comments. The media were not very complimentary about their old adversary, as there were dark rumblings around official council offices and committees.

I will let Mr E Barron, Jack's son-in-law, have the final word on Mad Jack Matthews, in a letter he sent to the *South Wales Echo* after the death of his father-in-law in July, 1888:

> *Whatever he has got in his house he bought honestly. He was a very eccentric man, for there was not a pawnshop in the town that he did not visit for the purpose of buying curios, watches, and such like. I have seen him go and buy a bag full of watches off Mr Blaiberg, Pawnbroker. He bought also old sticks, opera glasses, and old clothes. He was very fond of reading history, the lives of Wellington and Bonaparte in particular. He was very charitable, and passionately fond of children. I have seen him in one of his worst tempers cooled down by a child. So you see he was not all bad.*

A TYPICAL MAD JACK MATTHEWS ARREST AND COURT CASE

The early hours of 5th September, 1867, with no electric or proper gas lighting the streets were dark, very dark. The time, 1.45am and Police Constable James of the Cardiff Borough Police was patrolling the residential courts, the hovels and the dangerous alleyways surrounding them. There would have been hundreds of sailors in port visiting the brothels, drinking dens, and disorderly houses that were in the area surrounding Whitmore Lane (Custom House Street), and Bute Terrace. The pubs had closed some hours before but that didn't prevent street activities relating to alcohol and prostitution.

James walked up Charlotte Street and passed the *Flying Eagle*. As he did so he heard noises emanating from within and decided to investigate. The door was opened and the officer walked into the passageway of the pub. As he did so he was attacked by Mad Jack Matthews, who was either drunk or had entered one of his uncontrollable fits of rage, for which he was well known. The officer, not expecting the attack, was dragged into the bar by his collar, shaken violently and his head banged repeatedly against a wall.

To the layman it is difficult to comprehend why an officer sometimes does not fight back, man to man, straight away. An officer in those days, and indeed up until 1967 (when personal radios came in), was alone and the only aid for assistance was a whistle. A man assaulting an officer knew that if he could prevent him blowing a whistle it was to his benefit.

The suddenness and ferocity of the attack put the receiver on the back foot, allowing his attacker to gain an advantage. James was dragged back into the passage and kicked unmercifully before being thrown out into Charlotte Street. The officer could not gain access to his staff whilst he was inside the premises, and when he was on the street he drew it but couldn't use it. Matthews continued the assault, attempting to strangle the officer.

Coppers were tough men in those days, and as both parties fought it out, they used any methods they could to attack one another. The two men fought in the street and both subsequently fell at Whitmore Lane. Constable Perry arrived – probably the same Constable Perry who was later murdered in Cardiff, and to whom this book is dedicated. He would have known, as well as James, that Matthews was subject to violent outbursts.

Matthews was semi-conscious in the gutter but PC James had other problems. Jack's lady friend had turned up and was attempting to pull him to his feet at the same time fending off James who was trying to arrest him. Constables Perry and James pulled Matthews to his feet, screaming at the woman to go away. They dragged him, fighting all the way, to the police station where

PC Smith was on duty. The three officers calmed Jack down and at one point let him go as he appeared to have lost his aggressive stance.

All were breathing heavily, James and Perry were in a state of exhaustion. Letting a violent, arrested man go, leaving his arms free, not handcuffed, was not a good idea. Matthews threw a punch at PC James and then squared up to him in the police station. Unfortunately for Perry it was he who caught the next blow. He was hit on the side of the face knocking him against a table. With further assistance, the fighting man, who had lost his temper again was dragged into a cell and the door slammed.

Officers from the 1895 Bute Street Police Station would tell you that after a really bad altercation all that was needed was a rest, bandages, a mug of tea, and a coal fire. The prisoner had no such luxuries. His was a wooden bed with no mattress and no blankets. If the injuries were known to be serious a surgeon would be called, but no doctor would risk going in on his own with Mad Jack Matthews in such a mood.

At the court hearing on the 7th September, 1867, Jack's defence was that it was all the police's fault. PC James had come into his pub throwing his weight about, using obscene language and his manner was aggressive. Jack's defence solicitor questioned why this was, as surely a more reasoned and mature manner would have prevented his client from flaring up. He admitted Matthews was known to the courts for his bad moods but, on this occasion, he was provoked. He claimed that Jack had hardly touched the officer, it had been a weak attempt at an attack. He did admit to assaulting Constable Perry and for that he was sorry. James had wound him up and he was in a bit of a temper.

The local media then came in for a verbal lashing from Matthews' counsel. They were prone to denigrate and demean Jack Matthews in any way they could, building him up into a outcast and a thoroughly bad man. This injustice also infuriated Matthews to an extent that he wanted revenge on everyone who was making disparaging remarks and upsetting him.

It also seemed in one respect Jack may have been telling the truth on the night of the latest assault. James had denied using his staff on him even though Perry had intimated that James had indeed used his staff. Matthews body bore the marks of injuries that were similar to being hit with a staff.

Once again any police officer on his own with a 'madman', or who was known to have a violent temper, you had to strike first or as many times as you can, it is a 'dog eat dog' situation.

One can only imagine what the centre of Cardiff was like in the 1860s, maybe akin to Dickensian London with 200/300 drinking establishments packed into a very small area frequented by sad and impoverished people, together with alcohol charged sailors.

Some constables in that era were designated 'brothel detectives' and the intimation was, via Matthews legal representative, that he was targeted as such, especially as two of the three officers involved in the case were indeed 'brothel detectives'. They used to wind up his client, teasing him and hoping for a response.

Another storyline of events from another witness told a completely different tale. Living in the pub with Mad Jack Matthews at the time was Elizabeth Davies, who was said to be 'his woman'. She said she opened the front door of the pub at about 2am to let her dog in and Constable James entered at speed and grabbed Jack, who was in a downstairs room, and knocked him to the ground for no reason. A fight started in which the constable took hold of Jack and dragged him out into Whitmore Lane. PC James was staffing Jack across the body and was blowing his whistle. More patrolling police officers arrived and they dragged the man off to the police station. Police constables in those days were allowed to cross examine witnesses, this James did, but she did not change her story.

The magistrates found Mad Jack guilty on all charges. For the assault inside the Flying Eagle he was sent to the County Gaol for one month with hard labour. For the other assaults at the police station and on other officers he was sentenced to two months hard labour, both sentences to run consecutively. Matthews immediately started to shout at the magistrates. Fearing his temper the judiciary made a swift exit leaving the police officers to eject him from the Police Court and out into one of the holding cells to await transport to prison.

No doubt the bench holding the local press pack enjoyed the result which endorsed their branding of the man as evil and trouble. The papers were full of the trial and the sentence by the Court.

The police constables who patrolled Charlotte Street breathed a sigh of relief but the media probably could not wait to have him back again!

'Caged at Last' was the headline on the 7th September, 1867, then under the sub heading 'Revenge of the Brothel Detectives'.

Mad Jack seemed not to be the only publican who engaged in criminal activity. Michael Bryan's experience in the *Cork and Waterford* pub in Mary Ann Street is a good indication of the times. The year is 1859 and even at noon he was not safe as he was robbed within the pub by the landlady, Elizabeth Allen, and two others, one a labourer and the other a sailor. He was beaten unconscious and 7/6d removed from his pockets. The monies was spread around between the assailants. Michael Bryan lived in an adjacent street, Stanley Street, perhaps this was one pub he would never set foot in again!

The legendary stories surrounding 'The Madman of the Flying Eagle' will last. The exploits of the infamous often do. Minnie Maguire, who probably frequented *The Flying Eagle,* is another infamous character from that era. Her story is told in *The Cruel Streets Revisited.* Their names will go down in history. The names of everyone around them or who dealt with them will not!

CONTEMPORARIES OF MAD JACK: SAMUEL WILLIAMS AND PHILIP RICHARDS

Samuel Williams (top) and Philip Richards (bottom), publicans. Taken from contemporary newspapers.

Williams and Richards were pub landlords and contemporaries of Mad Jack but their lives were totally different. They were charitable men who lived clean and wholesome lives. One became the longest serving Cardiff landlord, and the other the oldest citizen of Cardiff.

Samuel Braunton Williams was a man who knew Cardiff well. The year is 1910 and he was then the oldest landlord in the city and soon to retire. Seventy years of age and most of it on the front line of Cardiff's streets. He was born in Barnstaple in Devon on 6th January, 1840 and had moved to fast-growing Cardiff with his family.

Like police officers, pub landlords see a side of life that many of us do not experience. A social gathering with alcohol-induced hilarity often leads to unruly behaviour and in Sam's day it was a powder keg of a society. He always tried to keep his pubs respectable and was a great friend of the local constabulary. Samuel was a disciplinarian and seemed not to welcome gangs of sailors off the ships. The *Temple Bar* in Bute Street, where he was landlord for many years shows his character and personality. It was situated in a rough seafaring area but he nostalgic and loved his locals and their stories. He positively promoted the 'same seat' style of landlording, i.e. each local had his own reserved stool or seat from where they could tell their reminiscences.

He made sure the *Temple Bar* was adorned with Cardiff-based oil paintings. Local pastimes such as badger baiting and cock fighting were seen as gentle hobbies and talked about with passion.

His previous public houses were not easy ones either. The first *Blue Anchor* in Wharton Street, *The Glastonbury* and the *Queens*

Chambers. He remembers ships unloading near Quay Street where Westgate Street now runs and one ship being unloaded where the local newspaper was printed.

Williams adorned his pubs with the trophies he had won for cock fighting, pigeon racing, and foot racing (running and walking races). He was described as a jolly man but was not to be crossed!

Sam was there when the Head Constable, McKenzie, read the Riot Act (this was an Act of Parliament dating from 1714 controlling groups of 12 or more, and led to the phrase about reading someone the riot act), from the steps of *The Royal Hotel*. His constables were trying to control a large unruly crowd that had gathered after Colonel Wood was elected an MP. The man he defeated died soon afterwards and the crowds that lined his funeral procession were just as big, but this time more respectful.

It is hard for any modern-day Cardiffian to believe that cows grazed behind the *Glastonbury* when Sam was the landlord. This pub was knocked down decades ago when the Butetown area was being redeveloped. It was a rough pub and police officers were often in attendance. Even in the 1960s it had its moments with trouble makers making a swift exit out of the back door on the arrival of the police, down the lane and onto Bute Terrace. It always seemed to flummox the serial troublemakers at that pub when the police entered via the rear exit, forcing them to run into Bute Street into the waiting arms of other officers.

Sam would have known Phil Richards who died in 1907. He was born in Penywain Farm, Roath in 1822 but the family moved soon after to Fairoak Farm not too far away. Shirley Road, Tyfil Place, and Penywain Road, now occupy the Penywain Farm lands and the Cardiff to Caerphilly railway line cuts a swathe through it.

Phil Richards had been the landlord of *The Royal Oak* and *The Blue Anchor* and he actually built *The Custom House* in Bute Street that many Cardiffians remember so fondly. The Cardiff Corporation had pulled down the previous *Custom House*. Many of the old publicans were charitable individuals. Phil Richards was one of the most respected publicans in Cardiff. He was the

Treasurer of the Ancient Order of Foresters, which gave him the honour of being the High Court Treasurer for the 39th Executive Council when, in 1873, it was held in Cardiff. He, along with Dr Samuel Wallace, founded the Widows and Orphans Society, which became a very successful branch within the Foresters and beyond. He died in his grand-daughter's house at 111, Monthermer Road, Cathays at the age of 85, at that time, Cardiff's oldest resident.

The aforementioned pubs were often rough places to be, with the local constabulary in attendance on a regular basis. We are very aware of how tough street life was for the police but it must have been pretty bad for landlords too. When trouble started, there was no phone to use to call for help, you did what you could and hoped that someone would run out and find a constable. If they didn't, you were on your own!

The memories of these two individuals of their associations, and their experiences would be a fount of knowledge to a 19th century Cardiff scholar. It was the most explosive time in the history of the town and they lived through it all.

CHAPTER TWELVE

"Revelation after revelation."
The Splott baby farmer

What is a baby farmer? The name refers to a woman, usually in the Victorian era, who agrees to purchase unwanted babies or young children from their mothers. An important part of the deal, if the baby was a newborn, is that the child needed milk, therefore the farmer may have been a wet nurse, or knew the whereabouts of a wet nurse to carry on her back street occupation.

Leslie James put an advert in local newspapers in the Cardiff area in 1907 wanting to adopt a baby. The advert was well worded and contained a box number for any enquirers to respond to. She did not use her lodging address of Portmanmoor Road, Splott. It was there she had taken rooms from the owner of the house, a Mrs Wilson.

There were several enquiries to Leslie's advert. It was a time when pregnancy out of marriage was seen as totally unacceptable and embarrassing. Childbirth was often covered up and the newborn secreted out of the public eye. There were many unwanted babies. Without contraception women became pregnant only to bring the child into a world of extreme hardship and poverty.

Emily Stroud was residing in Abertillery and was pregnant. The baby was unwanted and the advert was a Godsend, so she contacted Leslie James. The baby was born on 20th March, 1907 and was picked up soon after by James and taken to Splott.

A few months later a baby was found on the steps of a local Salvation Army hostel on Splott Road Bridge. Attached was a note allegedly from its mother stating that she could not cope as she was unmarried. The baby did not survive as it lay there for a while undiscovered, and sadly suffered from exposure.

A woman from Hengoed contacted Leslie James via the newspapers. Her name was Lydia English and she was very concerned about her sister, who was pregnant. James stated that she would come and fetch the baby as soon as it was born. The baby girl came into the world on 3rd June 1907 and it was with great haste that James was contacted to come and fetch it. The child's mother, Maud Treasure of Fleur De Lys who was unmarried, had custody of the baby girl for only one day, as on 4th June James travelled to Hengoed by train. The fee that the women had agreed for the baby was £8, a sizeable sum in that era for people living in impoverished communities.

English took possession of a receipt from Leslie James for the money. This receipt was later to be an important part of a police investigation. James, it was said, then conveyed the child back to Cardiff and to Portmanmoor Road. She subsequently sent letters to English saying how well the baby was being cared for and stated her intention of moving to the north of England in the future.

On 5th June, 1907, almost a month after taking possession of the Hengoed child, Leslie James had gone out in the evening to drink in the local hostelries. It would be imagined that the *Lord Wimbourne* in Portmanmoor Road may have been her local haunt. She returned to Mrs Wilson's lodgings very drunk, so drunk in fact that the landlady had to take her to her room and push her onto the bed. At the side of the bed the landlady noticed a small bundle and became immediately curious.

Whilst James slept the bundle was unwrapped and to the landlady's horror she discovered the decomposing body of a newborn baby. She ran out of the house and asked neighbours to run to Janet Street Police Station and fetch an officer. This was the first step towards a a trial that was to take the imagination of newspapers and the public by storm, not only for the morbid story of events, but also in its astonishing conclusion.

It was not long before Leslie James was arrested and charged with the murder of the infant. Her only previous conviction had been that of theft. James had sustained an injury in an accident early in 1907 and was treated at a workhouse infirmary. It seemed she had a changed personality after this bicycle accident and went on to steal property, something she would, it was claimed, never have done before.

Justice was indeed swift as the evidence against her for the murder of the Hengoed baby was heard in mid-June, 1907 at the Swansea Assize. More revelations were to follow.

Entering her plea of not guilty, James' advocate stated that the death was accidental, as the child had been unwell and simply passed away. However, the prosecution proved that the baby had been smothered and had died from asphyxia. The smothering of the child was a difficult one, was it accidental or intentional? A jury would find it very hard to convict in a situation such as that.

One of the many witnesses was Phyllis Watkins. She described herself as an Ensign in the Salvation Army. She stated she was the one who had that found the first baby on the steps outside her Salvation Army hostel. She told the jury the child was alive, and she had immediately wrapped it up in warm clothing. It was obviously ill and struggling to survive, so she took it to the Union Workhouse and into the custody of Doctor Edwards. He stated in court he did his best for the child but it died a week later, ostensibly from diarrhoea. He told the jury that it was definitely the diarrhoea that killed the child, his experience being that the condition was responsible for many a recent child's death. He also said in no uncertain terms that the period of time that the baby had laid on the steps of the hostel would not have contributed to its death, it was diarrhoea not exposure. Phyllis Watkins produced the letter she had found on the baby's body. This was to be important evidence relating to the handwriting when linking the baby deaths.

Another tale was told by a witness, Stanley Rees. He told the court that he was resident in Salford in Manchester. He had seen an advert in a Cardiff newspaper about the adoption of babies. He stated that he believed that a baby had been adopted by a Mrs Wilson at the request of Leslie James. It was from a house in George Street, Pontypool that the baby had originated at a cost £10, but actually only £5 had been paid as a deposit. The baby had been passed to the prisoner in Bristol. It all went wrong when the mother wanted the baby back.

There seemed no doubt in the minds of the judge and jury that Leslie James was acting as a baby-farmer, and while it was morally repugnant, it did not prove murder. At the conclusion of the first day's proceedings, the jury at Swansea Assizes were marshalled to the nearby *Mackworth Hotel* where they spent the night in isolation away from newspapers and unable to discuss the case with anyone. They had noted that Leslie James was not agitated and appeared very calm as she sat in the dock. There appeared to some people present to be an air of confidence.

What they had heard in evidence was a canny and very effective piece of police investigation considering the year and the state of forensic science at that time. A handwriting expert was called upon to give evidence. One could imagine how James felt when she heard his testimony. The expert said that the handwriting on the note left with the baby on the steps of the Salvation Army home and the handwriting on the receipts given to the baby sellers were written by one and the same person: Leslie James. This was damning.

The judge summed up the intricacies of the case by informing the jury the law was clear. If a person of sound mind killed another person with malice aforethought, that was murder. There was no question about the defendant's sanity. Her letters showed her to be a person of intelligence. If the jury thought she intended to kill the child, that constituted murder.

The jury retiring to consider their verdict, and spent only twelve minutes in the jury room. Returning, the foreman was asked whether Leslie James was guilty or not guilty on the charge of murdering the baby. Without hesitation the foreman replied, "Guilty." The judge spoke:

> *"Don't let anyone suppose that because you are convicted of murder that nobody pities you, nobody prays for you. I implore you to employ the short time that is left to you to prepare for death and for that mercy which you will undoubtedly find in Heaven, but which you cannot expect here. The sentence of the court upon you is that you be hanged by the neck until you are dead, and that your body be buried within the precincts of the prison in which you shall have been confined before your execution, and may the Lord have mercy on your soul!"*

But this was not to be the end of the case. There were revelations to come!

The court room was cleared and Leslie James was taken down to the cells and prepared for her removal to Cardiff Gaol to face her end on the gallows. It was the prison in Cardiff that had the facilities to accommodate females in the condemned cell, not all prisons had that facility. She had pleaded not guilty and consistently denied anything to do with the death of the baby.

The local council got involved as there were petitions being put together because of a general feeling that the conviction should have been for manslaughter and not murder. Numerous voters contacted their councillors showing their displeasure at the sentence of death. A few days before her execution her solicitor had received scores of letters begging him to do something and do it quick!

An urgent request was sent by the City Council to the Home Secretary, Herbert Gladstone, requesting the execution be delayed whilst an investigation took place. The petitioners challenged the murder convictions and its repercussions within Cardiff if a woman was sent to the gallows.

Several of the original jurors who sat on the Coroner's Inquest into the death of little baby Treasure also thought that the correct sentence should have been manslaughter.

The Home Secretary in London was unmoved. The sentence would go ahead.

More disclosures were to hit the streets of Cardiff via the newspapers that added to the interest in the case. Leslie James had appeared at her first hearing and charged with murder under that name. She had been arraigned and ultimately appeared at the Assize charged under the name of Leslie James. But on the day before her execution she admitted to her solicitor that she was not Leslie James at all, she was Rhoda Willis!

Sensation! The judiciary, the police and the general public were in a state of shock. There were serious questions to be asked of the system.

Leslie James was, in fact, Rhoda Leselles originally from Sunderland. She was from a good family who were so well off she was sent to a boarding school for girls in London. Her education was a good one and her future seemed secure, but on returning to Sunderland at the age of 19 she met Thomas Willis. He was a marine engineer, a job with some importance in the early part of the 20th century. It was a time of enormous growth in steamships and the port of Cardiff was a major centre of steam ship operation. The Willis family moved from Sunderland to Cardiff and took up residence in the Grangetown area of the city.

Tragedy was soon to strike the family as, soon after Rhoda had given birth to a daughter, her husband died, it was said of natural causes.

It was often noted that ladies in those days did not stay unmarried long, as the income of households were mainly the responsibility of the man of the house. So, it's unsurprising that Rhoda went to live with another marine engineer called Macpherson who lived in Paget Street, Grangetown. She had two daughters with him. For some reason their association did not last and Rhoda made her way to Birmingham, leaving the family at home in Paget Street. It was not long before Rhoda was on the move again back to lodgings in Cardiff. There followed bouts of heavy drinking.

Once the news was out that the judge had sentenced Leslie James to death and not Rhoda Willis, what else could possibly happen? Frantic alterations of official documents were undertaken under the auspices of police, prosecution, and defence attorneys.

Rhoda Willis then requested to see her ex-partner, Macpherson. The fastest form for urgent communications at the time was a post office telegram. This was dispatched to Macpherson and he, in a state of shock, duly attended at the condemned cell.

It was said to be a highly emotional meeting, with Willis crying and hugging the man. She handed him a letter exhibiting her regrets and begging him to try and keep the whole affair from their daughters, a request that appeared to be very difficult to accomplish. She signed her will and left the tiny amount of money she had to Macpherson to assist in the housekeeping of their two daughters.

One more shocking event was still to take place. Rhoda asked to see her solicitor on the evening of her execution, and this request was granted. Lloyd, the solicitor, arrived just after 6.00am on the morning of the execution, Wednesday 14th August, 1907 and spoke with the condemned woman. He was stunned by what he was told.

In spite of consistent denials throughout, Rhoda Willis then admitted she had in fact murdered the little baby girl and the jury had given the correct verdict.

The news leaked out. Everyone was stunned.

Rhoda went on to explain the circumstances of the death of the baby. She said she did not know why she smothered the baby, but she did so on the train somewhere between Llanishen and Cardiff. She had hurried the dead body back to her lodging in Portmanmoor Road and into her room where it had stayed until discovered by Mrs Wilson. It was wilful murder!

This revelation must have been a bolt out of the blue to Lloyd. Willis said the reason for her admission was to help him, the jury, and everyone else be content with the fact they had not sent an innocent woman to the gallows. Her death must not be on their consciences.

The infamous Pierrepoint Brothers were instructed to carry out the execution. They were well known in every prison, especially Cardiff, where they had worked many times before. They arrived at the prison on the Tuesday, the day before the execution. They went to the shed where the gallows was housed, just inside the prison walls. It was a well-trodden path for the Pierrepoints being very close to the prison's main gate. The shed was not visible from outside the prison as were other blocks that could be seen from the platforms of the Taff Vale and Rhymney Railways at Queen Street. Even today you can see into Cardiff Prison from this station.

It appears that the first thing the Pierrepoints did, after checking the paperwork, was to check the drop of the gallows compared to the height of the condemned woman. Then they checked the gallows were in perfect working order. The gallows in the Cardiff shed stood at the ground-floor level, therefore a person facing their end would stand level with the persons gathered to witness the event. The brothers opened the trap doors and saw that the pit below, which was brick lined, (similar to a modern motor car inspection pit), was clean and ready for use. They would have been informed that the condemned woman was just 5'2" in height meaning that a maximum drop of 5'10" was required. All was in order. All that was left now was the tying and securing of the rope.

At 7.00am on Wednesday 14th August, 1907, one hour before the execution, the Governor allowed the release of a number of prisoners early. The men and women should have waited until 8.00am for their release at the end of their sentences. It was decided that the two events, the releases and the execution, would clash and may cause problems.

One hour later, Rhoda Willis was walked from the prison block's condemned cell to the execution shed. One witness later mentioned how attractive she was. Another mentioned her golden hair glinting in the early morning sun.

She entered the shed and saw the gallows for the first time. It was said Rhoda appeared strong and mentally prepared for her death, although we simply don't know if that was the truth. The Last Sacrament was given by the prison chaplain. One wonders what her last thoughts really were as she stood waiting for the executioner to pull the lever that would open the trapdoor beneath her feet.

As was customary at executions, at 8.00am the prison bell tolled once to mark her passing.

All that was left to do was for the police to disperse the crowds that had gathered outside the prison walls, for the coroner to hold an immediate inquest into her death, and then to bury her.

The day of her execution, Wednesday, August the 14th, 1907 was Rhoda's 44th birthday.

CHAPTER THIRTEEN

The murder of William George Webb (11 months)

Bradford Street, 2017. The site of the grisly murder of a baby that brought residents flooding out onto the street in 1900.

David Hurricane Webb lived with his wife Minnie Frances Webb in Bradford Street, Grangetown. He had spent most of his life at sea but had managed to acquire employment in Cardiff working on a new dock. The couple had one son, a baby boy, whom they christened William George. Theirs was not a deliriously happy marriage, the husband claiming his wife needed direction and advice on many occasions. He had stated openly that Minnie was an awkward woman and needed some minor discipline, which he duly undertook as her lawful husband.

At 7.00am on the 14th December, 1900 he left home, as was the norm, to attend work. He arrived back at 5.05pm, again the norm. He noticed Minnie was not in the house and he asked his landlady, Mrs Baker, if she knew where his wife was. She told Webb that Minnie had gone out around ten minutes before he had returned.

He went upstairs to his rooms and saw his baby lying on the bed, apparently asleep. He lit a lamp and noticed that the baby's bedclothes had been turned down as far as his feet. In the light of the lamp, in the dark winter gloom, he saw signs of blood on his arm. He threw the light of the lamp on the baby's face. What he saw was hideous and caused him to recoil in horror. The child's throat had been cut across the neck, from one side to the other. It was so deep and forceful a cut that the head seemed almost severed from the body.

He ran downstairs and screamed at Mrs Baker, "My God, the child is dead, His throat is cut."

He ran out of the house to the Grangetown Police Station screaming, "Murder, murder. Police, murder!"

On hearing his cries, residents came out onto the street. It is said that the occupants of every house in Bradford Street were standing at their front doors or were milling in the road. Mrs Baker, the landlady, was outside of the house shouting, "Oh my God! Murder. Baby murder."

The desk officer had to calm the distraught man down in order to realise the gravity of the incident. It is probable that the desk man went outside the station and blew his police whistle as hard as he could in an effort to summon assistance.

Police officers ran to Bradford Street and made their way through the crowds of people that had now gathered. Meanwhile, the desk man at the police station informed the Detective Department of the incident.

David Webb ran to the bedroom with the officers and there, in the lamplight they saw the awful sight of the dead baby. Webb was taken downstairs by one officer and told to sit down. At that stage the officers could see that there had been a killing but did not know who had done it. Webb said it must have been his wife who was missing but no police officer goes on the word of one witness, perhaps his wife had been murdered too.

On William's bed was his bottle, partly consumed.

One officer, undertaking a quick search of the room, seized a cutthroat razor from behind a tin trunk that stood at the end of the bed and took it downstairs.

"It's mine," Webb said. "I keep it here, downstairs in the living room. It's usually in a razor box. It's been forced open."

A local doctor arrived at the scene and had to make his way through the crowd that had gathered outside Mrs Baker's house. The doctor had rushed up from the Clare Road surgery. He certified little William's life was extinct. He noticed there were three cuts to the throat. One stretched from below the baby's right ear to below the left. The power of the cut was such as to sever the windpipe and almost the head in front of the spinal column, which itself was partly severed. He noticed another cut below the main one about three inches long, and a further cut that had done damage deep within the baby's neck. He told the officers that there must have been considerable force used to achieve such injuries and with a very sharp instrument, probably a cutthroat razor. Arrangements were made to convey the body of William Webb to Bute Street Police Station mortuary.

With all the information gathered there was one vital question to be answered. Where was Minnie Webb? She was the key to the whole incident and the main suspect, there being no other evidence other than that from David Webb and Mrs Baker. A search commenced.

On leaving Bradford Street, Minnie wandered the streets of Grangetown, ending up in Holmesdale Street where a family acquaintance, Albert Shaldrack, who resided in Amherst Street, saw her. He had heard through the Grangetown grapevine of the death of the baby and knew the prime suspect was Minnie. He went up to her and enquired if she was alright, then asked if she knew what she had done. Minnie nodded in a positive manner, which prompted Shaldrack to effect a citizen's arrest.

He took her back to his home in Amherst Street. He sent neighbours for the police. Minnie told him that she had cut the baby's throat because she couldn't stand it anymore. She had tried to cut her own throat also. Albert noted a few shallow cut marks on her throat. She then told him that the quarrelling was getting worse between her and husband. He had beaten her that morning before going to work.

Inspector Durston was the first senior officer at the scene in Bradford Street. He heard that Minnie was in a house in Amherst Street and together with Chief Inspector Scott they attended. (For a full chapter on Inspector Scott's exploits see *The Cruel Streets Revisited*).

Artists' impression of Mrs Webb.

Minnie Frances Webb, (22), was arrested at 8.40pm on Friday 14th December, 1900 at Shadrack's home for the crime of murder. The arrest was undertaken by Chief Inspector Scott. She initially said, "I done it." She produced the razor from her pocket and said she had tried to kill herself also.

He told her formally she was being arrested and cautioned her in the usual terms: "Do you want to say anything? You are not obliged to say anything unless you wish to do so, but whatever you do say may be taken down in writing and given in evidence."

Her reply "I have nothing to say."

Minnie spent the night at Central Police Station until she stood in the dock at the Cardiff Police Court on Saturday 15th December, 1900.

The time: 11.00am.

The charge: "That she did on the 14th December feloniously and with malice aforethought kill and murder her infant child, William George Webb, aged 11 months."

The officer in attendance at Court was Police Inspector Butler. The Chief Constable, William McKenzie, was also sitting in the court room. It was noted by people in the court at the time that Minnie looked much older than her 22 years. Her stare was straight and her face showed no emotion. She was remanded in custody until the following Thursday and taken to Cardiff Prison.

An inquest, under the auspices of the coroner, was convened that afternoon. The time was 3.30pm and the officer in charge of the due process was again Chief Inspector Scott of the Cardiff Police Detective Department. Coroner Bernard Reese presided.

The first witness was David Hurricane Webb. In the dock was his wife, Minnie Frances Webb, their eyes must have met across the court room, One can only imagine what they were thinking as they stared at one another.

The coroner asked Webb whether they had quarrelled before work on the day his son was murdered. He replied that they had not quarrelled physically but had definitely had words together. He said she had acted strangely and "…had some very unusual times on her recently…", as quoted. William said he had tried to reason with his wife and coax her into behaving properly but it did not seem to work. He also told the court that his wife had never threatened to harm herself or their baby directly to him, but she had told her sister-in-law that one day she may "…do herself in."

He was also asked whether his wife fond of the child? His reply was guarded. He thought she generally was, but that she had "…the moods on her often." He also said that there was a tin in the bedroom in which his wife used to save pennies and halfpennies. It had been emptied on the day of the baby's death.

Mrs Baker, their landlady, told the coroner's court that she had never heard the couple arguing and, in her opinion, Minnie did not appear strange at all in her mannerisms. She noted that on Friday Minnie had been carrying the child about in the day as normal and had only left the house a few minutes before David had come home. One thing she had noted though was that Minnie had not lit the fire before her husband had come in from work, as was her usual practise. On several occasions, Mrs Baker was asked about Minnie Webb's care of the baby. She stated she appeared to love the baby and showed great respect for her own baby too.

The coroner asked Minnie Webb whether she wanted to ask any questions of him or the jury but she declined. The jury retired for just a few minutes before bringing in the verdict of wilful murder of baby William Webb. Minnie Webb was committed to the Assizes for trial.

One newspaper man at the court managed to have a word with a very distressed and emotional husband, David Webb. He told the reporter, "Minnie said that I beat her that morning, but I never did. All I have done is to try and keep her in a straight path as a decent woman."

On 20th March, 1901 Minnie Frances Webb appeared at the Glamorgan Assizes in front of Judge Bruce to stand trial for the murder of her son, William George Webb, aged 11 months. If convicted of murder the only option open to the judge was to sentence her to death.

Minnie pleaded guilty. The jury agreed, but the foreman stated that they all felt that at the time of the killing she was not responsible in her mind. The judge sentenced Minnie to be detained at Her Majesty's pleasure in a criminal lunatic asylum.

It was stated many times in journals of the day that detention in a criminal lunatic asylum was a fate *worse* than death. They were terrible places and many not fit for human habitation. Fear and violence. were a daily occurrence, not only perpetrated by inmates but by the staff themselves. It is not known what happened to Minnie Frances Webb and whether she was released into society again.

CHAPTER FOURTEEN

The 1975 Food College murder

Roath Police Station, 2017, largely unchanged since 1970s and indeed when it was built in the late nineteenth century.

To my mind, this ranks as one of the most unusual stories ever to come out of Cardiff. The story started in the north of England and was to end in a violent, pre-planned murder in a Cardiff college.

It was the day of the Police Promotion Examinations, Tuesday, 4th November, 1975. Constables had been studying for months in promotion classes in readiness for the Constable to Sergeant law tests. The examinations were not easy. An officer on the street had to make instant decisions on a variety of subjects from animal cruelty to murder, from gambling to domestic abuse, and he / she had to know their powers and the legislation surrounding them. An officer had to be a walking law book, the examination would test their knowledge to the full. There were three papers, Crime, Traffic, and General Police Duties. It was to last for most of the day.

There were so many officers taking the examination that a spacious hall had to be found. One such hall was within the Cardiff College of Food Technology in Colchester Avenue (recently demolished and replaced by housing). Desks and chairs were placed in the hall in long rows in readiness for the police invasion, albeit all officers would be in civilian clothes. Independent invigilators arrived first. Security was checked, examination papers were placed upside down on the tables, all was ready to go.

Scores of officers made their way to the college, in fact over one hundred, and they took their seats behind the single desks in the hall. There was the usual hum of pre-exam chatter, and banter until the chief invigilator shouted, "Settle down now. Quiet. Turn over your papers." The examination commenced.

Back at Roath Police Station in Clifton Street, Detective Constable (DC) 1491 'C' was in the deserted general office. He had already passed the examination and was to be promoted to Detective Sergeant the following year. Most of his comrades were at the college taking the examination, the only other detective officer in the station was the Detective Inspector (DI), an immaculate man and one not to be trifled with. He was the boss and everyone knew it!

The two CID vehicles had gone with the officers to the college. Extension 363 rang in the general office. It was the control room (CR)

"Who's that?" the voice at the other end asked.

There then followed a farcical conversation.

CR: "Get to the food college. Report of a shooting."

DC: "You're joking. It's a wind-up?

CR: "I'm putting your name down. I've informed you."

The DC went to the DI's office. The DI was even more disbelieving on being told there had been a shooting in a college full of police officers and used words to the effect of: 'Get out of my office you stupid person, It's got to be a joke."

To be fair to the Cardiff police service, jokes of that nature were unheard of but under the circumstances the information had all the hallmarks of a practical joke, or a malicious call.

The officer went back to the general office where extension 363 was ringing again.

CR: "Are you going to the bloody food college? They're screaming for the CID."

Retracing his footsteps to the DI's office, the DC received some more disparaging comments, before the simmering Detective Inspector and his Detective Constable left in the senior officer's car for the college.

Back in the college many of the officers taking the examination had heard a bang in another part of the building and sounds of shouting. The officers were ordered by invigilators to carry on with the examination.

As one officer said, "I just kept my head down and we did what we were told. We had no idea what was going on. Not an inkling."

Another officer said "It's a college, we heard some shouting but thought it was something to do with drama."

Another "If it was serious they would have stopped the exam. Everything carried on as normal. I was gobsmacked when I left the room and found out there had been a murder!"

Another "There was a bang and everyone stopped writing. Then one of the invigilators told us it must have been one of the *silence exam in progress* A-boards being knocked or pushed over in the corridor. So, we all carried on oblivious."

The most telling of observations came from two police officers, friends who were sitting near to each another. Both were firearms officers and one had represented the force at the Bisley Rifle range. Both officers owned shotguns and one was a top marksman and efficient in shotgun usage. One turned to the other and whispered, "That was a shotgun." His friend agreed.

They heard one officer from across the room shout, "Some bugger's chucked a firework. Bloody students think it's funny!" The two officers remembered staring at one another and shaking their heads in disbelief at this comment.

At that moment, the Chief Invigilator shouted, "Carry on. No noise. This is an examination room."

It may seem unbelievable, but not one police officer left the examination room. It was heads down and carry on. Prescript and discipline was paramount.

One officer commented afterwards, "Incredible as it may be, I wager whoever was in that hall at the time, would have carried on. We didn't have an inkling of the serious incident that taken place across the building."

So, what was happening that morning in the Food College?

As the Roath detectives arrived at the college they could see marked police vehicles dotted about the place, and students were leaving hurriedly. The officers were ushered to the bottom of a flight of stairs and there they saw the body of a man. There was blood on the floor and walls, and a shotgun lay on the floor nearby. A middle-aged man was standing next to the body. A uniformed officer was standing next to the man. The CID officers asked what happened.

The officer quietly answered, "He's just murdered him!"

The untroubled man standing next to the body was James Jardine Nesbitt, a 45-year-old nurse.

The murdered man's name has been changed for the purpose of this narrative. So, we shall call him Frank Thomas Francis. To add another level to the intrigue, Frank was formerly a long-serving police officer himself in Stockport until 1966. This previous employment had nothing to do with his murder though, it was his skill and expertise as a mountaineer that led to the gruesome event.

Frank was not just any mountaineer, but one who was well-known and respected as one of the best in Britain. His exploits were legendary and he had climbed with the most illustrious of British mountaineers. In the climbing community there are legends, Francis was up there with the them.

At the time of his death he was an instructor of a Cardiff remand home in Dinas Powys, and was attending a further education course at the college.

If only it had been known that the inconspicuous and unremarkable man who'd called at the college the day before on Monday 3rd November, 1975 had murder on his mind, the following sad events would not have occurred. The man in question, Nesbitt, had travelled up by train from the Exeter area, made his way to the college, and asked for Francis. He was informed that Frank was not in, but was in class the following morning, Tuesday.

He returned home by train and came back the next day, hiding under his coat a sawn off, over and under, Baikal shotgun. He made his way up the staircase near the main hall entrance, then to the first floor and tapped on a classroom door. It was opened by the lecturer and the man asked if he could speak to Frank Francis outside.

Francis came out and enquired what the man wanted. He was told it was important and could they speak together downstairs. Frank walked in front of Nesbitt, who he had never met before and did not recognise. As Francis was nearing the bottom of the first flight of the two-flight staircase Nesbitt took the shotgun out from under his coat, pushed it against Francis' back and pulled the trigger. The shot killed Francis instantly and his body tumbled down the stairs and onto the ground-floor corridor where it came to rest. The man followed the body down and stood next to it, placing the shotgun on the floor. He calmly awaited the arrival of the police.

There was some panic as the blood had started to flow and the shot had left its grisly marks on the stairwell wall. The man standing quietly next to the body appeared to some to have a calming effect.

The commotion at the time though was not allowed to be communicated to the officers in the main hall. The invigilators continued pacing up and down the aisles, ignorant themselves of what was going on.

The CID forensics scenes of crime were now *in situ* and dealing with the matter. College authorities barred students from passing through the corridor into which the stairwell emerged. Nesbitt was driven away to Central Police Station, CID General Office, and placed in an interview room.

It may be apocryphal but there is a story, (backed up by a detective who was there), that whilst sitting with the man a small insect landed on the interview table. The officer went to brush it off. The man reached across and held the officer's arm firmly, staring into the officer's eyes and said, "You should not kill God's creatures." The look was enough to unnerve the detective.

A psychiatrist, once the case was over, told this officer that the man was the type who could hold a grudge against someone for ever. Perhaps it was as well that he didn't squash the bug.

Nesbitt was later described as an honest and charitable man. Detectives from Roath who undertook the follow-up enquiries found that the man was so honourable he had even applied for a shotgun certificate as he did not want to break the law in his murder plans!

What had happened? And why was Francis so brutally murdered?

James Jardine Nesbitt's background proved he was highly

educated, a graduate with a science degree from a Manchester technical college. Nesbitt joined the merchant navy and became a second engineer but left to further his career working on communications on a nuclear submarine.

Then something happened. Nesbitt became confused and faced a moral dilemma. The catalyst possibly came when he was offered promotion and he realised that his responsibilities could involve the mass-destruction of human life. He was employed on a submarine carrying nuclear weapons. This he simply could not come to terms with, so he left his employment.

It appears he became obsessed with charitable work and the furtherance of young people's education. He took a role as a mathematics teacher in 1966. He raised money for charities and gave several thousands of pounds from an inheritance to charity. It is said that a chunk of his monthly income also went to charity.

He obtained a job in at a care home in Windermere, in the Lake District, as a nursing orderly. This was to be a crucial step on his path toward murder.

One of the patients was sadly suffering from polio. The patient was Dorothy, the wife of Francis. In 1972 Frank Francis had been employed as an instructor in an outward bound school in Devon. He had lived there with Dorothy, who was confined to a wheelchair. Michael Grandon (not his real name) was the senior instructor at the school and there was a good professional and personal relationship between the two men. Grandon was seemingly after a senior mountaineering certificate and to this end they both went to a hazardous peak, Gillercombe Buttress, in the Lake District. Sadly, during the climb Grandon lost his balance and fell to this death.

After the tragedy, Francis returned to the outward bound school in Devon and commenced a close friendship with Michael Grandon's wife, eventually leading to a relationship. This may have started some tongues wagging.

A cordial relationship blossomed between Nurse Nesbit and patient, Dorothy Francis and the conversation turned on several occasions to the untimely death of Michael Grandon. Whatever happened during those conversations it appears that Nesbitt got it into his head that Grandon's death was not an accident, even though it was deemed as such by a Coroner's Court. No blame at all had been attached to Frank Francis.

Nesbitt then visited the parents of Michael Grandon and found them also unhappy with the manner of their son's death. This led Nesbitt to becoming even more obsessed with the idea that Francis was implicated in Grandon's fall. Nesbitt moved away to take up a job at a psychiatric hospital in Devon, but his obsession that a wrong had been done got stronger.

The result of the Grandon inquest seems to have been totally ignored by Nesbitt, even though it was a thorough and proper enquiry. In the later court case the prosecution barrister stated, "...there was not a shred of evidence..." that could implicate anyone in Grandon's fall and death. This was after a full and comprehensive police investigation.

Nesbitt joined a gun club in Exeter and purchased a Baikal double-barrelled shotgun. He had his licence application ratified by a magistrate. There was nothing to say that Nesbitt was anything other than a normal citizen with a penchant towards shooting. No-one had an inkling that this was to be more than a hobby. In his garage, he placed the barrels of the shotgun in a vice and hacksawed them to a length where he could easily conceal the weapon under his clothing. He also changed the stock of the weapon and affixed a smaller handle that increased its mobility.

He went back to see Grandon's parents again early in 1975 to discuss the tragic accident once more. He had clearly become convinced that Frank Thomas Francis had somehow been involved in Michael Grandon's death, even though there was no evidence! By now Nesbitt's self-appointed social conscience was working overtime. The overwhelming thought that an injustice had been done was burning away inside him and he knew he had to be the judge and jury to rectify it.

Meanwhile, Francis was continuing his employment at the

centre in Dinas Powys and to further it he agreed to take on a 12-month course based at the Cardiff College of Food Technology in Colchester Avenue. Nesbitt discovered where Francis was working and in October, 1975 he called at the centre and asked for Francis. He was informed that Francis was not there but on a long-term course based at the Food College. Nesbitt returned to Devon and his job as an assistant nurse at the Exe Vale hospital.

In the following month, on Monday 3rd, November, Nesbitt travelled to Cardiff and to the college. He asked for Francis but was told he was away for the day and back tomorrow. So, once again Nesbitt returned to Devon.

Making the trip again on Tuesday, 4th November, Nesbitt found Frank Francis this time in the lecture room. Nesbitt asked for Francis to leave the room as he wanted to talk to him. Neither man had met the other before. As Francis was walking down the stairs Nesbitt took out the shotgun and held it against the man's back. Firing a single shot, he killed the man instantly. Officers remember that the shot was so powerful that were pellets deeply embedded into the stairwell wall. They had passed through Francis who now lay at the bottom of the second set of stairs, at ground floor level. Nesbitt placed the weapon down and stood next to the body.

A member of staff at the college approached him and asked what happened. Nesbitt said, "I shot him. He killed a friend of mine."

Teams of Cardiff detectives spent time in Devon and the Lake District discovering the background to the murder. Nesbitt told the Detective Chief Inspector in charge of the case that it was not possible that Grandon could have had an accident and there must have been some other reason he fell to his death. The detectives could find no evidence that Francis was involved in the death of his friend. The inquest was conclusive, it was an accident.

The team in Devon interviewed numerous people, delving into the background of Nesbitt. It was found he was charitable, friendly, and extremely honest. However, in Nesbitt's trial the judge and jury heard how the man was mentally unstable and a paranoid schizophrenic. Doctors warned of the danger of ever releasing Nesbitt back into society as he thought he had done nothing wrong other than right a wrong. He lacked any sense of remorse for his crime. He was sent to Broadmoor Hospital for an unlimited period.

James Jardine Nesbitt died in the Exe Vale County Asylum Hospital, Exeter on 4th March, 1982. Ironically, this was the same hospital he worked in.

To quote a Detective Sergeant involved in the investigation, "If Nesbitt had put the gun back under his clothes and simply walked out there would have been very little chance of detecting that murder. There was no CCTV in those days, his description would have been circulated, but being a Devon resident he was unknown to the Cardiff police. He had no previous convictions and was a law-abiding man in a professional job." Perhaps the officer is right, but we shall never know.

The final word comes from the detective constable at the Roath Police station who drove the sceptical Detective Inspector to the murder scene. "I still think of it, but it is the memory of my boss shouting at me and telling me it was a wind-up that will live with me for ever. Some wind-up!"

CHAPTER FIFTEEN

Llanishen (1844): the death of Elizabeth Sullivan

The parish of Llanishen, four miles north of Cardiff centre, was once the most rural of areas. Today it is made up of residential estates, schools, shops, and pubs like any other city suburb. If you live in Llanishen have you ever wondered what was on the land your house now occupies? Have you ever thought, "What happened here?" It may be that the little bit of land you now inhabit was once occupied by someone else in the mists of time. The Llanishen Story is one of injustice, inequality, poverty, and hurt.

In 1844, the Irish were flooding into Wales to escape the death-dealing potato famine. Many who had crammed into the ships were unaware that they were heading for even more hardship when they arrived in Wales!

Some worked on the docks, some laboured in heavy industry, some laboured in the fields, and all for a pittance in pay, especially if you were a woman. There were so many incomers that employers could pay the most meagre of wages. Destitute immigrants had to take whatever they could get.

Llanishen did not escape this human tragedy as women and their families moved inland from the docksides in an attempt to survive. It is quite sobering to think that the fields that now are housing estates and roads were once populated once by hundreds of Irish labourers and their families.

Elizabeth Sullivan was 35 years of age when she gravitated to farmland in Llanishen searching out, with her husband and young son, work that could pay enough to feed themselves. Desperation drove them to a local pasture owned by Farmer Langley, a Llanishen churchwarden. They spoke to one of Langley's foremen, Calahan McCarthy. He had worked at the farm for about five years and lived in a tiny cottage on his employer's land. It was he who offered Elizabeth and her husband a job and told them they could work for 6d (2½p) a day, included lodging. Elizabeth picked up the potatoes her husband had dug.

They were shown their new hut, it was more like a large pig-sty. It was later described as suitable only for animals to inhabit, but to Elizabeth it was a roof over their head and somewhere to rest. The hut was already occupied by Daniel Sullivan and his wife, among others. Little did Elizabeth know that during the next few weeks other impoverished workers were to live in the tiny hut alongside them. At one time it was said to have ten occupants, all of Irish origin, men, women, and children. Some spoke no English or Welsh, only their native Irish tongue.

Elizabeth worked in the fields of Llanishen, bent double, for twelve hours a day, picking up the potatoes and putting them into large baskets which she took to a central collecting place. For much of the time it rained, but if she did not continue working she would not get paid, so through the most atrocious weather she worked the fields. Elizabeth had also been thrashing corn, a very physical and demanding job for a man, let alone a malnourished woman. Outside their pigsty she would light a fire and boil potatoes for the family and other residents.

Potatoes were her staple diet, a fare she was well used to. Life was hard, very hard, and it was having an effect on Elizabeth's health. The long autumn and winter months of 1844 were bad and the fields were a bitter place to be.

Elizabeth Sullivan was ill, she could hardly bend to lift a potato basket, let alone thrash hay, her strength was limited to just standing or walking, but without working there would be no money. She became so ill she could only crawl.

Calahan McCarthy tried to help by attempting to feed her some bread and milk he had purchased. It was difficult for anyone to assist, as no money was being earned when not hard at work.

None of the Irish newcomers seem to have heard of 'relieving officer', a man with medical experience who was employed by the parish to care for the illnesses of the poor who could not afford a doctor. One wonders if any doctor could have done anything for Elizabeth, as one day she was so weak she could not even make her way out of the hut. She lay on wet hay hoping for a miracle that never came. Coughing and delirious Elizabeth was dying, like thousands of others of her countrymen and women during that terrible time. The squalid, damp, rat-infested hut was accelerating the poor woman's demise.

For her fellows living in the hut her state had given them another problem, what to do with her when the inevitable happened. They were staunch Roman Catholics and had to have Elizabeth's body disposed of according to the strict rules of their religion.

It was said that Farmer Langley's son was keen to get rid of people like Elizabeth as they were trouble and potentially an expense they did not want. It appears that the Llanishen parish officers were not keen to pay for pauper's funerals either, but that was denied at a later Coroner's Court.

Elizabeth's husband lifted Elizabeth onto an old cart and they made their way to Cardiff. They had worked out that if they left the parish of Llanishen and headed for Cardiff help would be given to them. The woman was partly covered, it was raining, the Llanishen lanes were muddy and boulder-ridden. Her husband and others were pulling and pushing the cart as it passed other Irish labourers working in the fields for other Llanishen farmers. Perhaps they thought that one day it may be them on that cart. Elizabeth's journey was a travesty of social justice. There were things that could have been done, if it suited the landowners.

The cart and its sad cargo gravitated to an Irish immigrant area in Stanley Street, Central Cardiff, in what was described even then as "…a miserable row of hovels at the back of David Street." They paraded Elizabeth up and down the street, hoping that someone would take her in. After around ten minutes someone did indeed take pity on them. A woman named Ryan, who was as poor as a

Stanley Street. In 1844, when Elizabeth was brought here, it was mostly Irish-populated. Photo taken from Bute Terrace, just prior to demolition of St David's Church in the 1970s.

church mouse herself, saw the state of the woman's body and offered to take it to her house at 10, Stanley Street.

Stanley Street had suffered long and hard from cholera outbreaks with rooms and outbuildings occupied by suffering people. Defecation piled up promoting insanitary conditions and further spreading cholera.

Another view of Stanley Street.

Mrs Ryan then sent for the relieving officer for St John's parish, who duly attended and gave relief in the form of a 6d piece to the persons who had accompanied Elizabeth in order to get food. The woman was carried into the Stanley Street house and given some bread and milk. Doctor Bowen attended and ordered that Elizabeth be given regular drinks of milk and brandy and fed with broth if she could take it. He diagnosed that she was in a state of exhaustion brought on by hard labour and malnourishment. For two days, the local Irish people tried to do what they could to help, but it was to no avail. On Sunday evening Elizabeth Sullivan passed away. Doctor Bowen certified the death.

There was a strong feeling of animosity towards the Llanishen landowners who, according to some at the Coroner's Inquest on Elizabeth, thought that the atrocious conditions, accommodation, and work practices must have been known and therefore tolerated.

It was also said that many of the Irish immigrants who were working in the fields of South Wales were being forced out with their dead to take them to other parishes to save money. The parishes of St John's and St Mary's in Cardiff were the prominent two that families headed for.

The coroner and jury were obviously deeply moved by the sad death of Elizabeth Sullivan, which they thought could have been prevented. They demanded to see in the witness stand both Farmer Langley senior and his son. It was the senior who turned up and appeared in Court.

There were dire warnings by the coroner that a manslaughter charge could be the end result, considering the circumstances involving Elizabeth's demise. Mr Langley intimated that he was not aware of the plight of the workers on his land and his son, Francis Langley, was more aware of their actual working practices.

Members of the jury were allowed to ask questions as they were obviously concerned as to why and how such things could happen. Why was it that these poor people were being directed to the Cardiff parishes and not remain at Llanishen for treatment?

It was explained that Irish people did not like to attend the workhouses, they preferred to look after their own in their own way. Also, they were not made aware of the help they could have obtained from the relieving officer, who had the power to advise a workhouse to take sufferers such as Elizabeth.

The constituents of a manslaughter charge were debated and in the view of the coroner they were all present in this particular death. It was thought the son, Francis, should appear in Court to answer questions. Mr Langley senior stated that it may be impossible for him to do so, but after further questioning stated that he could get Francis to the court within two hours.

The coroner made a ruling that in this case it was not going to be necessary to see his son, but gave a dire warning that if future cases came before him with similar circumstances there would be a manslaughter charge to answer.

Prior to Elizabeth's death, a note dated 8th January, 1841 had been written to Mrs Davies, supervisor at the workhouse, by Dr James Lewis. It contained instructions to workhouse staff should Elizabeth Sullivan be admitted from the house at Stanley Street.

> *Mrs Davis have the goodness to wash the poor Irish woman, Mrs Sullivan, with soap and water and put her comfortably to take her medicine as directed. Two tablespoons, three or four times a day. Her diet will be gruel and arrowroot, with a dessert of gin or brandy in it, three or four times a day.'*

The court's verdict was that Elizabeth Sullivan died of great exhaustion, brought on by a long sealed disease called Ague (a fever or shivering fit), and a want of proper nourishment.

Whether the Langleys were cruel or just unaware of the suffering of their workers, we shall never really know. What is apparent is that Irish immigrant labour was a cheap asset to farmers in Llanishen who took full advantage of it. The fact that farmer Langley senior was a churchwarden and aware of relieving officers and help for the poor, surely indicates a callous disregard of human suffering.

That was then, this is now. Thankfully times have changed. The extreme social iniquities suffered by the desperate lower working classes in Wales were thankfully to change but not before thousands perished in poverty.

APPENDIX

Tiger Bay Gold

Tiger Bay woman and Tiger Bay man,
Tiger Bay grandad and Tiger Bay gran.

Tiger Bay black and Tiger Bay white,
Tiger Bay left and Tiger Bay right.

Tiger Bay tears of Tiger Bay joy,
Tiger Bay girl and Tiger Bay boy.

Tiger Bay young and Tiger Bay old,
Tiger Bay coal and Tiger Bay gold.

Tiger Bay whimper and Tiger Bay roar,
Tiger Bay less and Tiger Bay more.

Tiger Bay mosque and Tiger Bay church,
Tiger Bay found and Tiger Bay search.

Tiger Bay dog and Tiger Bay cat,
Tiger Bay thin and Tiger Bay fat.

Tiger Bay climb and Tiger Bay fall,
Tiger Bay short and Tiger Bay tall.

Tiger Bay happy and Tiger Bay sad,
Tiger Bay good and Tiger Bay bad.

Tiger Bay yours and Tiger Bay mine,
Tiger Bay's gone into Tiger Bay time.

JOHN F. WAKE
2017

ACKNOWLEDGEMENTS

The author appreciates the assistance of the following individuals and organisations in the compilation of this book.

Cardiff Libraries.
The Cathays Heritage Centre Library staff.
Jill Emery and Brian Lee for invaluable archive assistance with reference to 'Mad' Jack Matthews.
Tom Page Research, for his ongoing investigations into the births and deaths of many of the persons named within this book.
Dai Thomas for his assistance on the family history of Constable Kingdom.
Mark and Paul Hinge.
The Glamorgan Archive.
The Cardiff City Police Archive.
The Virtual Museum of Police in Wales (Facebook) and Ross Mather.
South Wales Constabulary.
Welsh Newspapers Online.
Caroline Maiorano, The *Packet Hotel,* Bute Street, Cardiff.
Martine Lloyd.
Jimmy Dukes.
John Blackburn.
Mal Bosley.
David Norrington.

Printed in Great Britain
by Amazon